Break the Bricks

Break Through

To Find the Real You

LEN TRAN

Break the Bricks

First edition September 2023

Jacket design by Hoang Vi Kha

Manufactured in the United States of America

ISBN: 979-8-9869102-3-9 (paperback)

ISBN: 979-8-9869102-4-6 (hardback)

Library of Congress Control Number: 2023916539

DEDICATION

Lara and Leo

Virginia Shorin Ryu Karate

To all those who are ready to discover their true potential

ACKNOWLEDGMENTS

This book would not have been complete without the support of my beautiful and lovely wife, Kelly (Phuong Linh) Tran. Thank you for always believing in me! To my daughter, Lara, and my son, Leo, thank you for being patient!

Thank you to my karate students at Virginia Shorin Ryu for believing in my teachings.

Author's Note

My entire life has been filled with countless challenges and difficulties, some of which appeared to be insurmountable at the time. My resiliency was put to the test, and I was motivated to discover new methods to conquer these obstacles. Some of the challenges were external, such as financial or societal impediments, while others sprang from inside, in the form of negative attitudes and limiting views that I held about myself.

When I look back, the challenges that existed in my mind were usually the most difficult to conquer. My struggles with self-doubt, anxiety, and insecurity kept me from realizing my full potential. It was a never-ending struggle to put an end to the critical thoughts that kept running through my mind and to have faith in my capabilities.

Through adversity and struggle, I found solutions to these challenges. I immersed myself in the study of psychological underpinnings of ideas and actions, gained an understanding of how the brain functions, and reprogrammed my thinking that each failure is a set up for success. I worked on being more conscious, having more encouraging conversations with myself, and recasting negative ideas into beliefs that empowered me. I learned the importance of establishing objectives that are attainable, dividing those goals into more manageable chunks, and rewarding myself for making progress along the way.

During this voyage of introspection and maturation, I realized that the lessons I've learned along the way may be useful to others going through similar situations. Sharing my discoveries with the world gave me a profound feeling of purpose. I did it with the hope that it would motivate and enable others to triumph over challenges they face and lead the life they envision for themselves.

In this book, I offer my narrative, along with the lessons I learned and the tactics I devised to overcome hurdles and unleash my real potential. I want to use this opportunity to urge you to accompany me on this journey of self-discovery, and I hope that the words I share may provide direction, motivation, and the encouragement you need to triumph over challenges encountered in your life. Always keep in mind that you can conquer any challenge and do everything you set your mind to. Have faith in yourself and allow me to accompany you in this life-altering adventure.

"Close your eyes, clench your fist, and hit those bricks.
Sounds easy, but it's a challenge that sticks.
Where's my courage, my strength, my might?
They're here but hidden out of sight.
Take a breath, slow your count, focus on the bricks.
The answer's within, it's where it clicks.
You're tougher and stronger than the bricks.
Ready to go, with all your tricks?
Concentrate and Break the Bricks!"

—Len Tran

CONTENTS

Introduction

As you prepare for your next event, you cannot tame the thoughts running in your mind that you are not capable, others are better than you, or worse yet, what others will think if you fail. The more you think about it, the more the impostor syndrome takes control. Fear and doubt make you preoccupied with failures rather than triumphs. Eventually, your mind conjures images of you throwing in the towel before the event occurs. What is the reason you are torturing yourself? You are not the only one fighting with this invisible enemy running in your mind. You are your own worst critic! It is common for us to show empathy for others, but for ourselves, we tend to be more judgmental.

In this book, *Break the Bricks*, I share my experiences as well as years of studying human psychology for people of all ages on the factors that keep you from reaching your full potential. I've found a method for tapping into your subconscious mind and rewiring your beliefs so that you can become the best version of yourself.

As you read this book, take time to focus on the insights in each chapter. Doing so will allow you to take a deeper dive and unearth prior occurrences that will help you comprehend and solve the problem, making your route to success clearer. Of course, there will be challenges ahead, but you will grow by reflecting on what has transpired. There are two ways to live your life, in my opinion:

1. Live in the present moment to cultivate a sense of peace and happiness.
2. Live with a purpose to create a sense of direction and fulfillment in your life.

To achieve your objectives or aspirations, you must be willing to create opportunities. Whether it's to become a successful CEO or to accomplish a small goal, you need to put in the time to learn and grasp the nature of goal setting. In other words, whatever you intend to achieve in the future, you must thoroughly prepare. Everyone's path to success is unique, but surely there is at least one rocky one. Don't be discouraged since each hiccup is an opportunity to learn something new. Why? As much as you want to succeed on the first try, failing is just as important to gain confidence. On the bright side, you can always correct your mistakes. You know how to mend that previous rocky road if you find yourself in the same circumstance.

Break the Bricks is intended to help you overcome difficulties and begin living joyfully. When you look at others and think they are better than you, it is because you haven't allowed yourself to see how excellent you are. You contribute uniquely to society. Someone well-known on a global scale does not mean they can connect with everyone. Your mannerisms, approach to business, or words of affirmation can have profound effects on others.

This book is divided into three sections in which you will discover how to better understand yourself, prepare for action, and finally, rise to take action. Remember, the biggest hurdle is the one you create in your mind. Be ready to accept challenges and become the finest version of yourself. While you may praise and credit others for their abilities, don't forget to acknowledge your own as well. In short, whatever bricks of barriers you have met in the past or will face in the future, use the three sections in this book as tools to shatter them.

PART 1

KNOWING YOURSELF

1 Feeling Lost and Stuck

"I want to see if I can. I don't know if I can. I want to find out. I want to see. I'm going to do what I always do: I'm going to break it down to its smallest form, smallest detail, and go after it. Day by day, one day at a time."

-KOBE BRYANT

Feeling Stuck in Life and How to Deal with It

D o you have the impression that your life is not going in the direction you want? Do you feel lost and have no idea what to do next? If your answer is yes, then it's time for damage control. Not knowing how to cope with those feelings of being stuck, useless, or confused can be destructive. It will surely drain your energy, causing you to get submerged in the muck. The more you become preoccupied with these sensations, the more you will develop sentiments of worry, dread, and exhaustion.

During my first job working as a chemical engineer in Long Island, New York, I experienced these sentiments for the first time. My routine at work consisted of arriving at the office, punching the time clock, changing into my overalls, and then passing through two doors before entering the clean room. Inside the clean room, there were a few testing apparatuses for distinct types of filter membrane testing. My job was to assemble the apparatus and then sit there to monitor how much the filter membrane captured dirt particles. As I sat there watching the computer monitor display how much dirt the membrane collected, the thought of waiting for forty-five minutes for the process to complete made me wonder if I could have done something more productive in the meantime. Once the testing was done, other similar tests ensued throughout the remainder of the day.

After working there for three months, I felt trapped. I questioned whether this was indeed the path I wanted to take. Seeing my peers work on more interesting projects made me want to be on their team. I considered asking my manager for permission to join them, but I doubted whether I was technically qualified or even on the same level as my coworkers. I was unsure of what I genuinely wanted to do. In the end, performing the same unpleasant assignment despite my best efforts left me exhausted and uninspired.

Why Do We Get Stuck?

You become stuck when you begin to feel uneasy; you are perplexed and question whether you should become someone you are not. When words like "should have" or "could have" enter your head, you start comparing yourself to other people who you think are more capable. Comparison suffocates confidence! The more you focus on others, the less you focus on your strengths.

Back when I was in high school trying out for the tennis team, I made the same error, allowing my emotions to take over since I fueled myself with a negative perspective. On the first day of the tryout, I was first in line to begin the drill with the coach. I was so enthusiastic that I went for every ball that came my way. For long balls to the baseline or short balls near the net, I was confidently crushing them. Although there were a few balls that sailed outside the line or missed the target by a few feet, my pride wasn't affected until a six-foot tall guy with long blond hair and a bandana walked onto the court. He looked like Andre Agassi, one of the top

American tennis players in the 1990s.

"Ready to hit some balls, Adam?" the coach asked as Adam approached the baseline. Adam nodded and braced his legs in a ready position. As the ball was tossed, he planted his foot and hit the ball exactly back to where the coach wanted it. No matter where the coach fed the ball, he let his body create all the force, making every stroke so flawless and on point, with relaxed shoulders and wrists. I was impressed by Adam as I completed laps around the tennis courts per the coach's instruction.

"All power is based on perception. If you think you've got it, then you've got it. If you think you don't have it, even if you have it, then you don't have it."

-HERB COHEN

After watching Adam hit every ball so neatly in whichever direction he desired, I convinced myself that I should give up tennis since I would never be as good as Adam. When it was my turn for a second round, I got to the baseline, but this time my confidence shrunk like cashmere in the dryer. I lost the desire to pursue the balls. All I could think of was Adam's talent. I ended up making even more errors than I did in the previous round. Worse yet, Adam stood at the baseline watching me make erroneous shots. I had given up hope of making the squad by the conclusion of the tryout.

Being stuck begins with your thoughts. If you believe you are trapped, then you are trapped. Your circumstances are the result of what you put in your mind. What you read, what you listen to, and what you think shapes your personality. These factors will eventually become your new paradigm.

Get Unstuck and Move on With Your Life!

By getting rid of negative ideas that are running through your mind and replacing them with positive ones, you will start to see a whole new world that is full of options and possibilities. Put an end to the statements "I can never have that" or "I can never be like that," and start asking yourself, "What can I do to have that?" or "What can I do to be like that?" Give yourself the opportunity, the potential, and the belief to attain what you want. You will be astounded by what you can do. Bear in mind that if others can accomplish their goal, there is a good chance that you can as well. The journey may be challenging, but if you put in the effort, you will find a way.

Here are some strategies that could help you unchain yourself from being stuck:

> **Let Your Mind Wander**
> When you realize that someone else has superior abilities than you or that the challenge at hand is insurmountable, your mind will frequently give up. That's okay; just let it be! Your brain functions in this way; it is meant to protect you from perceived potential threats. The brain is only able to carry out the processes that are absolutely required when in survival mode. It does not accept fresh information and does not preserve it in the long term. Give yourself a couple of days or so, and then, when you are feeling comfortable and attentive, boost your mind with willpower and get rid of that old sense of being stuck in a rut.

> **Have Fun with It**
> It has been demonstrated that taking pauses as you struggled is an effective method for recuperating from the negative effects of stress, which, in turn, may enhance both performance and mood. Getting over the effects of stress at work may help recover one's energy and mental clarity, which in turn reduces feelings of exhaustion, as well as the

risk of sleeping disorders and cardiovascular disease. Therefore, regardless of how hectic your life is, permit yourself to be free from your work, your duties, and those annoying errands for a brief period. The easiest way to de-stress is to go for a stroll outside, breathe in some clean air, and listen to soothing music. Even better, if you don't already have a pastime, start looking into getting one. Learning how to strike a balance between your personal life and your professional life is not only good for your health but also offers another way out of a rut.

> **Keep A Journal**
Writing your objectives and tasks is a great approach to boosting self-confidence and holding yourself accountable at the same time. Keeping a diary is a self-care exercise that is useful by people ranging from scientific geniuses to contemplative artists. I have one as well, and I frequently add new entries or keep tabs on the ones I've already written. By doing so, I get myself back on track whenever I stray off course. Keeping a journal also enables me the advantage to look back and observe the progress I've made toward achieving my goals. This method can serve as a useful tool for assessing your development and progress regularly. The most essential thing is that it can bring you joy and pleasure to see how much you have overcome challenges. Both Leonardo da Vinci and Albert Einstein kept journals in which they detailed and illustrated their remarkable ideas and creations. You never know what kind of fantastic thoughts or ideas may come to mind when you let your thoughts wander freely while writing.

> **Talk It Out**
Start by sorting through your list of friends, mentors, or someone you feel comfortable with sharing your frustrations or thoughts. Similarly, in a therapy session, talking out your thoughts can help you feel relieved from your unsolved

problems or doubts. Sometimes, hearing yourself speak out loud is better than listening to that little voice inside your head. It makes you realize that the situation is not as bad as you think. Moreover, hearing different perspectives from trusted ones has its benefits. It might help you view your problems differently. If you didn't talk it out, you would probably still be focusing on the problem rather than trying to find a solution.

➤ Geographically Change Your Location

Alter your environment to alter your state of mind. If you do not like where you are now, it may be time to relocate. The decision to move was a challenging one for me. Since I immigrated to New York City from Vietnam at the age of eight, I have been accustomed to everything in my environment, including my community, my friends, and even the hectic pace of city life. Nevertheless, I wasn't happy with the job I had at the time. Because there were no prospects to advance in my work, I had the impression that I was approaching a stalemate in my professional life. I was aware that I needed a change, but it was difficult for me to move away from this comfortable environment. A considerable amount of time passed before I ultimately forwarded my resume to an agency in Virginia. After receiving a call to schedule an interview, I traveled to Virginia within the next three days and was extended a job offer within the following week. After weighing all the benefits and drawbacks of the new work and exploring the nearby area in Virginia, I concluded that I would have a brighter future there. Following the completion of my resignation letter and packing my belongings, I bade farewell to New York City. In hindsight, choosing to move was one of the wisest decisions I had ever made.

"You are the average of five people you
spend the most time with."

-JIM ROHN

> ### Surround Yourself with Quality People
> Your circle of friends constitutes a significant portion of your surrounding environment. They can be the source of strength, self-confidence, and comfort. On the other hand, they can cause you to feel inferior, psychologically stalled, and embarrassed if with the wrong crowd. In a nutshell, they have the potential to either help you grow or set you back. Therefore, carefully consider who you want to include in your most trusted inner circle and choose them accordingly. Eliminate any connections that are unbalanced since they will only bring you more pain in the long run. If you've discovered that other people are taking more than giving, it means they are stealing vital resources from you without replacing them. Toxic negativity is another pitfall. Keep your distance from those who continually provide you with counterproductive input. You will acquiesce to their comments, and becoming unambitious and insignificant is a likely outcome of this negativity. Since humans are social beings, it is essential for everyone to surround themselves with other people to develop their interpersonal ties. Nevertheless, the secret to success is to surround oneself with the appropriate company. To get started, go over the list of individuals that are currently in your life. Honor those who are contributing positively and minimize interactions with those who take vitality from you.

> ### Avoid Analysis Paralysis
> Analysis paralysis is the act of thinking and mulling over possibilities excessively to the point that nothing gets started. Too much analysis about which appropriate action to take or a desired outcome is counterproductive when it

comes to completing objectives. Studies in psychology and neuroscience demonstrate that analysis paralysis has a significantly larger toll on your productivity and well-being than just lost time.

I have been teaching karate to adult students for over seventeen years. My brother, who is also a martial arts instructor, teaches children. I noticed a distinction between children and adults in that adults have a propensity to overthink situations. As a result, by the time they have finished evaluating, the interest in carrying through has finished as well. The kids, however, follow exactly what they are taught. They waste no time thinking since they want have fun while training.

As for my students, when I teach them new techniques or sequences, I receive many questions, not only about the order in which techniques are performed but also the purpose of each motion. No matter how many times I tell them to focus on the pattern of the sequence first, they continue to examine and question before putting it into practice.

According to the findings of a recent study conducted at Stanford University, published report in Scientific American magazine on May 28, 2015, Grace Hawthorne, a professor at the Stanford University Institute of Design, and Allan Reiss, a behavioral scientist, collaborated to find a way to scientifically measure creativity using brain imaging. They came to the conclusion that excessive thinking not only impairs our capacity to carry out cognitive activities, but also prevents us from realizing our full creative potential.

These findings suggest that overthinking a problem makes it harder to do your best creative work. The best way to combat analysis paralysis is to stick to the main goal and not overthink things. When you find yourself overthinking, just pause for a minute and tell yourself, *I need to decide and it's going to be the best decision based on the knowledge that I have.* For example, if you are given a task and you find yourself stuck with having too many ideas to start, go with your first instinct. Usually, your first instinct is your best one. Having two ideas at once is setting yourself up for ambivalence, leading to paralysis by analysis.

2 Past Experiences Can Stop You or Start You

"I've missed more than 9000 shots in my career. I've lost almost 300 games. Twenty-six times, I've been trusted to take the game-winning shot and missed. I've failed over and over and over again in my life. And that is why I succeed."

– MICHAEL JORDAN

Use Failures as Fuel to Move Forward

If you have fallen short of your goal, don't feel bad. It means you are getting close. The question is, have you picked yourself up and tried again, or chosen to remain down and hold out hope that one day you might be able to get back up? Well, if you have gotten up to continue your quest, congratulate yourself because you are on the right track to achieving what you set out to do. However, if you are still down and feeling defeated, it's time to pick yourself back up and try again. It is understandable how unfortunate events from the past or repeated failures might negatively impact your thinking. The realization that you are unable to surmount that challenge once more will take you on an emotional rollercoaster. Therefore, you need to flush all those feelings down the toilet since life is all about facing new challenges, learning from your mistakes, and moving on. You cannot let the past hold you back.

It takes a lot of guts to admit defeat, especially when the reasons were due to circumstances beyond your control. Confront the issue head-on and stop looking for other people to shoulder the responsibility. The sooner you come to terms with it, the faster you will move on. A few years ago, I was requested to give a presentation at my workplace to overseas customers. I looked over the materials that had been sent by the organizer so that I could be as well prepared as possible. On the day of the presentation, I went over the company's characteristics and highlighted the most important advantages by using PowerPoint™ slides. Around the midway point, I became aware that most of my audience was gazing at me in a perplexed manner. Even though they had headphones on and were listening to the translator, it was clear from their expressions that they could not understand what was being said. I was at a loss for what to do, but I had to continue completing the presentation. During the questions and answers segment, customers asked how the attendees would benefit from my presentation. My head spun, and I wondered if the translator sufficiently conveyed the meaning of what I said during the previous sixty minutes. As they continued to press me for answers, I realized the presentation I had given was off-subject. I tried to respond to as many of their questions as I could to make up for the hour that they had wasted listening to me. Then my allotment of time had run out, and it was now the next presenter's turn. I couldn't stop thinking about what an idiot I looked like on that platform, so I made a beeline for my department as soon as I could to demand answers from the organizer about why I was given improper materials. The event organizer pointed the finger of responsibility at me, saying that I should have requested the appropriate presentation slide deck instead. I knew the blame game was in play. Instead of back and forth, I decided that it was fruitless to continue the argument, but instead find ways to make myself credible again.

*"Mistakes are always forgivable if one
has the courage to admit them."*

-BRUCE LEE

I was aware that a contributing factor to my failure was not asking the organizer the required questions before presenting. Despite this, the harm was already done, and it was time for me to rectify the issue. In addition to that, I didn't want the people who came to see me to walk away unhappy. Since it was an all-day event, I went to my manager and requested that I be given a do-over on stage so that I could correct my previous performance. It was fortunate that my supervisor was able to find time for me, and I was able to provide the content that my customers were expecting to hear. The approval and admiration that I received from my audience brought a sense of fulfillment to me, but what made me happiest was that I didn't allow my previous setback to discourage me. I recognized that setbacks are unavoidable in every endeavor, regardless of the motivations behind them. Even the most skilled Olympians can make mistakes, such as having a false start, which might result in disqualification. Nevertheless, when a mistake occurs, you need to put an end to your self-pity, fuel your focus, and rise back up.

How Are You Getting Back Up?

*"If you fall, make sure to land on your
back because if you can look up, you
can get up!"*

-LES BROWN

When things don't go your way, these are the questions you need to ask yourself:

Do I let my mistakes weigh me down?

Do I get more knowledgeable because of what I learn from my mistakes?

Do I wish to have greater adaptability as well as increased resilience?

Successful individuals, whether professional athletes or leaders in business, use their setbacks to develop momentum rather than to slow their progress. Therefore, when you run into problems, immediately move on to the next stage of the strategy.

Create a "Get Back Up" Plan

For every goal you have or every dream you chase, infuse your mind with the understanding that challenges and hindrances are waiting for you. Be prepared for the damage that these stumbling blocks could inflict. Acknowledge and be willing to accept that there will be setbacks and disappointment. Regardless of how large or tiny they are, they have the potential to bring you to your knees and cause you to fail, but if you know how to turn them to your advantage, they are the power that will make you thrive. The path to success is never simple. You are going to have mishaps, and you will wonder whether you want to go down this road. However, if you allow challenges to deter you, you will never have the chance to learn who you are or your potential.

My tennis instructor from high school told me all the time, "Quitters never win, and winners never quit." Therefore, even if I was going to lose my battle, I would make it a point to ensure that my opponent beat me rather than I beat myself. This was the case even if I was ready to lose.

Your backup plan if you fall:

> ### Your Failures Are Your Journeys
> The journey through life is unique for everyone. Some people like taking a path of least resistance, while others actively seek out difficulties because personal development brings joy. Nevertheless, regardless of which way you proceed, never allow yourself to wallow in your misery simply because others have had it easier than you. Every individual has his or her unique blend of experiences, situations, challenges, and chances. In your own time and at your speed, you will arrive at the destination you envisioned. No matter how long it takes, the most important thing is how eager you are to accomplish the goals you have set for yourself.

> ### Have the Courage to Stand Back Up
> It is simple to throw in the towel when faced with a challenge. Pause for a moment and ask yourself: *What was the motivation for getting started in the first place?* There is no denying that falling short in front of your loved ones or friends may be a source of both sadness and humiliation, but they are not the reason you embarked on this adventure in the first place. YOU ARE! You are the one who created this dream. Step up, accept the challenge, and make your dream come true. Explore the depths of your being to unearth the motivation behind how greatly you desire to achieve this dream. Muster the strength to pull yourself up by your bootstraps and demonstrate to yourself that you are more resilient than the person you were the previous day.

"If it doesn't work,
change the attitude, don't change
the destination."

-LEN TRAN

➢ **Being Persistent to See Growth**

The process of flourishing takes time and effort. To truly realize how far you've come, you need more than the passage of time. When my children practice piano, they often get bewildered. Seeing their expressions, I know the only way for them to improve is through the struggle of learning and practicing. I am aware that the road to achievement is never an easy one. There are undoubtedly many circumstances in which you must force yourself to feel uncomfortable to experience growth and gain knowledge. Consider going to the gym as an illustration. It might be intimidating to lift huge weights, and especially when you're on your last repetition, you may question whether you should go back to the gym the next day. However, if your goal is to increase the size of your muscles and your strength, going back to the gym and continuing with training is a must. Put the proverb "no pain, no gain" into practice, and you will find that the payoff is well worth it.

➢ **Revisit Your Coaching Journal**

Earlier, I had suggested keeping a journal to write down your goal and see your progress. Take one step further and divide the page into two columns. Title the left one with "Current Obstacle," and list the things that are holding you back. Title the right one with "Options," and these will be the choices you can make to face the obstacle. This will provide a clearer vision of how to overcome those obstacles.

Here is a sample of how I organize my journal for my own growth. I also use this format when coaching clients for goal setting.

My Coaching Journal

Today's date:

What do I want to accomplish?

Why is this important to me?

When should I meet this goal?

Who is the person who can help me achieve my goal?

What are some of the indicators to show that I am on the right track?

How would this goal make an impact on my life?

On the next page, I list Obstacles and Options.

Obstacles	**Options**
What are the current obstacles?	What are my options to tackle this?
e.g., Feelings, Thoughts, People, Surroundings.	

Keep in mind there is no such thing as failure; it is an experience. Permit yourself to be propelled forward by these experiences each time you find yourself on your back.

"Don't ever be ashamed of the scars life has left you with. A scar means the hurt is over and the wound is closed. It means you conquered the pain, learned a lesson, grew stronger, and moved forward. A scar is a tattoo of a triumph to be proud of."

-UNKNOWN

3 Understanding Your "Why"

"Champions aren't made in gyms. Champions are made from something they have deep inside them—a desire, a dream, a vision. They have to have the skill and the will. But the will must be stronger than the skill."

– MUHAMMAD ALI

Your "Why" is Important

W *hy do you want to do that*? Whenever you are asked this question, you should be able to answer without hesitation. Understanding your "why" is truly an essential element to propelling yourself to another level in life. Make that "why" become your passion, your craving, and eventually your purpose. Most importantly, revisit your "why" frequently.

Have you ever wondered what your reasons are for getting up every day? Everyone is going through each day searching for their "why" just to find the purpose of their existence. Some might stumble in their searches, while others make successful discoveries.

While chatting with some individuals on various occasions,

it occurred to me that certain people prefer a simple life with no challenge. They are content with whatever each day has offered them. Is it wrong that they live that way? Definitely not if they are happy with the life that they have chosen to lead. Everyone has their way of living. You are ready for a change, ready to take a step further to flourish your personal development and transformation. Do not let yourself be stuck in a rut in any aspect of your life, whether it be your career, relationships, or your creative ideas. Unleash your life's calling and fill it with thrilling experiences and new discoveries. Let's uncover your "why" in the same challenging way that my dad and I did many years ago.

In 1982, a few years after the end of the Vietnam War, my father and I, along with twenty-three other people, fled our homeland in the hope of finding freedom and a better life. We were crammed into a tiny fishing boat to the point where the water's surface was less than a foot lower than the edge of the vessel. It was decided that two boats would set sail at the same time, and our boat would follow the other. However, because of the mayhem that occurred before dawn, the other boat left too early. We had to escape as fast as possible before daybreak so that we wouldn't be caught by the Viet Cong of the new communist dictatorship. Unable to locate the other boat, we became disoriented since they had the compass. We had no option but to use the sun as our primary means of navigation in the hope that we would be found and rescued by another nation. After being lost at sea for five days, we ran out of fuel, food, and water. We lost hope and were on the verge of giving up since there was no sign of being rescued. Some cried as death awaited us, and some yelled, wanting to go back to Vietnam. Chaos broke out when fear and despair took over. At that moment, my dad screamed, "We need to stay the course. We are going to make it." The entire boat quieted. My father's comment was a gentle reminder of the reasons why they set out on this adventure; the "why" they decided to get on this boat in the first place.

In a matter of minutes, everyone mustered their will to live even though they were starving and extremely thirsty. We got the impression that we had succeeded in overcoming the obstacle. However, not long after, a foreboding storm cloud moved in our direction and threatened to capsize our boat in a blink of an eye. I glanced at my father, and for the first time, I saw him visibly shaken. He clasped both hands together to his chest and prayed, as did everyone else on the boat. That foreboding cloud moved faster and more vividly toward us. The force of the wind made the water pound on the wooden hull of the boat, sending salty spray into the air. The wind shrieked and roared in our ears, but we drowned it out with our loud prayers as the boat tossed and turned on the raging sea. We braced ourselves while clinging to the wooden frame of the boat as we prepared for what we thought would be our last moments. Suddenly, I felt water drops on my face and when I opened my eyes, I couldn't believe what I saw. No more storms, no more wind, but rain! Just what we needed! I gathered some of that precious water in the palms of my hands and drank it. Everyone was overjoyed and searched for jars to fill with rainwater in preparation for the days ahead. After about five minutes of pouring rain, the dark cloud broke up and was replaced by the sun. We were terrified that mother nature would swamp our small boat amid the South China Sea; yet, instead of drowning us, she showered us with life in the form of rain sent down from the sky.

We persevered on our journey using the precious rainwater, as well as food and fuel donated by a few fishing boats that we had encountered at sea. They were aware that we were boat people and needed assistance. On the twenty-first day, we were rescued by the Hong Kong coast guard and brought to shore, thanks to the goodwill of those people as well as our determination to live. The journey we took via the South China Sea to find freedom was very hazardous. We might have been slain by pirates, or we could have died of malnutrition, dehydration, and storms, but because of our "why," we mustered the fortitude to fight against all odds to remain alive and eventually made it to our intended destination in the United States.

"If you can't figure out your purpose, figure out your passion. For your passion will lead you right into your purpose."

-BISHOP T.D. JAKES

Knowing Your Why and Purpose

Knowing your life's purpose has several advantages and benefits:

- More opportunities and financial stability
- A longer life
- Strong mind and body
- A stronger immune system
- Lower risk of developing dementia
- Increased resilience
- More confidence
- Greater focus
- More fulfillment
- Confidence in making decisions

Over the last three decades, I've made it a priority to train in Okinawan karate under the direction of my sensei, who is a highly respected instructor. My sensei stressed how important it was to have a distinct goal in mind when training in this kind of martial art. To begin, my response was straightforward: to enroll in a self-defense class. Having said that, as time went on and I advanced my karate training, my purpose broadened and became more logical.

Today, the reason I train in karate is to become more disciplined and focused as a martial artist. I've come to realize that the ability and mentality I acquire via karate have a noteworthy influence on other elements of my life, including career, business negotiations, relationships, and family life. My karate training has enabled me to develop mental and emotional fortitude, tenacity, and self-mastery via the practicing of discipline and attention. In every aspect of my life, martial arts training has ingrained in me the capacity to remain cool under pressure, to make choices that are in my best interest, and to have a keen sense of resolve and purpose.

When I reflect on my several trips to Okinawa, Japan, to learn karate, I'm thankful for the many life lessons I've collected along the way that go well beyond the physical methods. For me, it has turned into a way of life that molds my personality and provides strength to develop into a more improved version of myself. I have decided to continue training in karate with the same steadfast goals: to foster self-discipline, concentration, and personal development, not just on mats in the dojo, but in every facet of my life.

As I progressed further in my training, I also expanded my knowledge of the Japanese language. One term in particular, "Ikigai," stood out to me as remarkably interesting. It conveys the notion of "a reason for being" and stands for the inherent value or purpose that endows one's life with meaning and makes it worthwhile. How this idea might be applied to one's regular activities struck me as perceptive.

Ikigai is a Japanese concept that essentially mean "to find that which makes life truly worthwhile," and I've adopted it as a guiding principle in my life. Ikigai provided a framework for making choices and creating objectives that are in alignment with my genuine purpose, as well as assisting me in reflecting on my personal beliefs, interests, and talents. I have found that by implementing the idea of Ikigai into my day-to-day life, I have been able to acquire clarity, direction, and a feeling of satisfaction in pursuit of activities that are genuinely important to me.

Whether it be in my karate training or other aspects of my life, I make it a goal to live in line with my Ikigai, meaning that I aim to engage in pursuits, cultivate relationships, and achieve objectives that provide pleasure, meaning, and a sense of purpose.

Ikigai has been a potent reminder to live honestly and purposefully, as well as to continually seek and cultivate those aspects of my life that bestow genuine worth and meaning on my existence.

How can Ikigai help us be fulfilled?

Rules of Ikigai:

1. Stay active
2. Leave urgency behind
3. Eat only until eighty percent full
4. Surround yourself with good friends
5. Maintain health with gentle exercise
6. Smile and acknowledge those around you
7. Be with nature
8. Be grateful
9. Be present
10. Live your Ikigai

Incorporating these guidelines into your life can provide you with an increase in energy and enthusiasm to pursue hobbies and ambitions. In essence, these guidelines serve as a guide to help achieve your goal. You'll be unstoppable after understanding your mission. You'll be able to mold your life in whatever manner you choose if you have a laser-focused attitude and clear objectives. You will no longer wake up in the morning wondering what to do since your mission will present a clear sense of direction.

A well-defined mission provides meaning and motivation, moving you ahead with unyielding commitment. Mission motivates your actions and choices, providing a feeling of purpose and satisfaction in whatever you do. With this clarity, you'll be able to direct your energy and efforts with steadfast concentration toward your objectives, overcoming barriers and pushing through restrictions.

You'll uncover new levels of productivity and success as you connect your life with your mission and maintain a laser-focused attitude. You'll have a powerful sense of purpose, providing you with the tenacity and desire to overcome obstacles and persist when facing adversity. With a clear sense of purpose, you'll be able to design your life into the form you choose, resulting in a meaningful and purpose-driven existence.

"Your purpose in life is to find your purpose and give your whole heart and soul to it."

-BUDDHA

When you have a clear understanding of your life's mission, you have a stronger reason to work toward achieving your objectives. There will be times when you get distracted, whether it be due to social pressure from your peers, which causes you to deviate to a new route, or due to your mind attempting to prevent you from venturing outside of your comfort zone. Nevertheless, you should maintain your concentration on your "why," determine its significance, and give it your whole heart and soul. You will have the ability to ignore all hindrances and concentrate on your objectives.

In my first year at college, my mind was set on chemical engineering as my major. On the other hand, most of my friends were majoring in computer science, and they frequently tried to persuade me to switch my academic focus, arguing that the employment market for computer science graduates would be more expansive than for any other engineering majors. Additionally, it would be more enjoyable to spend time together while studying if we did so. I was nearly persuaded to change my major after hearing those extremely convincing arguments. Having said that, after considering why I do what I do, I was led back to my passion. After coming to terms with my decision, I ignored such comments and focused on achieving my objective. Because I stood my ground, it saved me from wasting money and time. When you have a firm grasp on your "why," you won't spend time pursuing objectives that don't matter.

How to Find Your Purpose

Here are some ways to find your "why" and to help you begin the process of uncovering your purpose in life:

> **Identify Ways You Make People's Lives Better**
  In 2005, my karate school began at a local gym near my workplace. At first, I invited a small group to join me in a practice session. Instead of lifting weights, I entertained them with a few karate moves. After convincing them how karate would be beneficial physically and mentally, they decided to give it a try. Amazing progress was made after a few courses and word of mouth. More individuals began approaching me about taking the course. Since I was fortunate to meet my karate instructor who trained me at no charge, I decided to follow suit by teaching for free. These students have continued to train with me for over seventeen years, and I'm honored to have made a difference in their lives. Changing people's lives is an experience for which I have no words to explain. Don't squander your chance to create a positive impression on someone. It's nice to have something, but it's much better to give something.

> **Do What Makes You Forget About Time**
  Regardless of how much time passes, nothing is more important to me than being with my loved ones. I didn't have the benefit of my mother's presence in my early life. I was separated from her at the age of seven when my dad and I fled Vietnam as "Boat People." It took me eight years to finally reunite with her and my five siblings. I always wished I could go back in time and reclaim the time I spent away from her as a child. Therefore, now that I have a family of my own, I want to spend as much time as possible with my

wife and children. I don't want my wife and kids to go through what my dad and I went through. Whether it was reading bedtime stories, hitting balls on the tennis court, or helping with a science project, those were times I cherish most in life. If you're doing something that makes you feel good instead of something that drains your energy, you're on the right track. When you follow your calling, you never feel lost.

"Life is not measured by the number of breaths we take but by the moments that take our breath away."

-MAYA ANGELOU

> ## Even If You Look Like a Fool, Do It
Before you can become an expert in anything, you begin with minimal competence or knowledge about what you are doing. Once you decide to continue an activity, you will make mistakes and possibly embarrass yourself along the way. This is called passion because these activities are meaningful enough to you that you don't care about other people's opinions. You accept and are willing to appear as a fool so that someday you will be a graceful master. The more intimidated you are by a major life decision, the more you probably need to continue doing it.

> ## What is It about You that Draws People In?
There is a reason why you are a source of energy that people want to be near you. Perhaps it is your charisma or the answers you provide that give comfort and security to others. Sometimes you don't see your impact until someone comes up to you and say, "I like the way you approach things and are proactive in solving problems." By hearing these words,

you determine your strengths, and you can certainly tie this to your "why." It is one thing to know what you want to do, but it's a nice affirmation to hear from someone else that it is your calling.

➤ **What Would You Do If You Had a Year Left to Live?**
It is rather sad to use this scenario, but at the same time, it brings out the realization of how short life can be. Most people don't like to think about death, but only when facing death do we focus on what is profoundly important to us. Studies have shown that people generally don't regret the things they did but regret the things they didn't do. Therefore, don't hesitate or hold back; shoot for the stars. Live every day as your last day so you won't have self-condemnation. Find your sense of purpose and stop struggling with what is important to you or what your values are. If you are not living for your values, then whose values are you living for?

➤ **If You Could Teach Someone, What Would You Teach?**
This question probably triggers you to think about how you can pass on your knowledge and wisdom to others. When I met one of my first karate teachers in New York City at the age of nine, he kept saying, "I am teaching you karate so you can maintain a healthy body and mind, not to fight." Every Saturday morning, he stood in an open grass field at a botanical garden and waited for kids to arrive. Since we all came from poor families, he didn't charge us. His dedication and purpose were so strong that making money was not his goal, yet his passion was to change the lives of us poor kids.

4 What Are Your Gifts?

"The person born with a talent they are meant to use will find their greatest happiness in using it."

– JOHANN WOLFGANG VON GOETHE

We Are Born with Gifts

There will be times in your life when you wonder what it is you are skilled at doing. The answer may not be easy to come up with given that it is human nature to judge ourselves in relation to others. This is logical since you may believe other people are better positioned in life than you. Unfortunately, this course of action is both counterproductive and pointless. Seventeen years ago, I applied for a leadership position with my employer. Aware of the people who also applied for the positions, I couldn't help but feel anxious, thinking I was less competent than they. As I filled out the application, I couldn't shake the idea that other applicants had more impressive credentials. My mind became consumed by those thoughts, and questioned whether I should maintain this frame of mind. Even after I submitted my résumé, there was uncertainty. A few weeks later, I got a phone call from Human Resources scheduling me for an interview. Naturally, I was pleased, but the happiness didn't last long before those doubtful thoughts crept into my mind again. Doubts spoiled a moment of happiness for me. On the day of my interview, there were three reputable directors and two supervisors who sat in front of me. Looking at them gave me further cause for concern. Even though I was nervous, I did my best to provide answers that were accurate and based on my expertise. Two weeks later, much to my astonishment, I received an offer for the position.

One month into working with my new colleagues, I realized the people whom I compared myself to were no different than me. We were just as lost with the new working process. As we tried to figure things out, I recognized we each had our specialty when it came to our managerial roles. My colleagues excelled with organizational goals while I concentrated on my employees' personal goals. In working with my employees, I learned to listen and relate to their frustrations and desires. That was when I discovered my gift—I was able to inspire through deep listening and help them discuss their fears and doubts. While my colleagues were good at meeting goals, I excelled at propelling others and helping them overcome their obstacles.

We all have skills that define us. Our talents form a lovely and varied world. Don't compare yourself to others or worry about other people's skills. You risk overlooking your talents if you compare too much. You can make a difference by embracing and nurturing your abilities; recognizing both your strengths and flaws to sharpen your skills. Recognition implies being real to oneself without adapting to society or seeking affirmation. Enjoy your successes, great or little, without comparing them to others. Understand that everyone has distinct skills and abilities that make the world so varied. Comparing oneself to others distracts you from your own journeys and contributions. Instead of being envious of others' capabilities, concentrate on your strengths and interests.

With focus and patience, you may develop your specialty. Strive toward your objectives without being influenced by others. Knowing that your abilities are worth exploring, you may follow your interests with delight and excitement.

Discovering Your Gifts or Talents

Experts in the field of coaching and psychology agree that to become proficient in any activity, a minimum of ten thousand hours of practice is required. Do you believe, however, if you had the talent, there is a chance this time may be reduced by fifty percent? Over my forty years of training in various forms of martial arts, I have encountered a wide variety of individuals and situations. Some people have trained for years but are still unable to execute techniques properly. On the other hand, some started not long ago but are able to understand concepts and quickly progress to the black belt level. The only plausible explanation is that these abilities were present in them from birth. Participating in activities that are novel and difficult is the best method to get insight into the skills and abilities that you possess. The best way to discover your potential is to get to know yourself and accept the challenge of confronting the unknown. When I first became a supervisor, I had no idea I had any impact on my employees. If I hadn't applied for that job, I never would have had the opportunity to learn about my skills and capabilities. Therefore, don't fear trying new things. Push beyond your comfort zone so that your abilities may shine and you discover your full potential.

Ways to find your gifts:

> **Talk to Those Who Know You Best**
> Family members or friends closest to you know you the best. Ask them for their sincere opinion on what they think are your unique qualities. What would you say are the most exceptional things you've done up to this point? Additionally, try to recall any aspects of your performance that garnered the greatest praise from them. Nevertheless, check to see if any praise you received was consistent and related to the tasks you accomplished. Compliments should come from the heart and not out of politeness.

"You never know what you can do until you try, and very few try unless they have to."

-C.S. LEWIS

➤ **Just Do It!**

Do not hesitate to try new things; this is the best way to determine whether you are excellent at anything. In the worst-case scenario, you will discover you are not that good and go right back to where you started. Vice versa, you might end up surprised by what you can do, and a whole new universe opens before you. Therefore, for any new thing that is introduced to you, don't be afraid to give it a try. There is nothing to lose and a lot to gain from an opportunity given to you.

My daughter, Lara, has a passion for singing but only sang in the confines of our house. She was afraid of being in the spotlight. One day, we went to a party hosted by a friend, and they had constructed an impressive stage, complete with a karaoke system. I asked Lara to choose her favorite song to sing for the audience. She declined kindly while anxiously gazing at the more than fifty people gathered there. Because I understood how she was feeling, I stopped trying to convince her and gave her time to gain her confidence. After waiting for half an hour, I inquired once again. Lara reconsidered after I encouraged her to "just do it" since she needed to demonstrate her abilities on a more manageable platform before moving on to a larger one. Her performance left my wife and I astounded. It was perfect in every way. Her beautiful voice was a gift from God.

➤ **Relax and Reflect**

Take a moment to unwind, relax, and think. Remember back

to a time when you engaged in an activity and time was not a pressing concern. If it seemed like time passed quickly that you didn't even realize it, there must have been a rational explanation. When you cease paying attention to your surroundings and instead concentrate only on the activity you are engaged in at the moment, this is known as "zone out." It indicates you take pleasure in what you do and you appreciate doing it. It is why artists spend countless hours completing their work and why engineers persist on a design of his or her creation until it is finished. Even though there was no deadline, these individuals stayed laser-focused on their tasks. They worked until the wee hours of the morning, staying awake all night. As you reflect, you will realize you have another talent or skill that should be brought into the light and shared with the world.

Working on Your Gifts and Talents

"The artist is nothing without the gift, but the gift is nothing without the work."

-EMILE ZOLA

Your abilities have the potential to advance you in a variety of ways, from the acquisition of new possibilities to the accrual of more financial gain. If you can cultivate and properly develop your abilities and talents, you have the potential to bring wealth beyond your wildest dreams.

*"I've always believed that if you put in the work,
the results will come. I don't do anything half-heartedly
because I know if I do, then I can expect half-hearted
results."*

-MICHAEL JORDAN

Michael Jordan is known for having a legendary level of work ethic. His teammates witnessed how strenuously he trained and the persistent toughness that he brought to each game. Michael Jordan was born with a talent for basketball, but he never stopped working to improve his game and become an even greater player. Dean Smith, head coach at the University of North Carolina (UNC), when interviewed in the documentary *The Last Dance* said that Jordan was "inconsistent as a freshman," but his work ethic stood out. He also stated that Jordan was one of the most competitive players on the team when he joined the squad, and highly motivated to improve his skills. The ability to always push himself to improve was Jordan's notable talent. He shared his aspiration with Roy Williams, an assistant coach, that he wanted to be the most accomplished basketball player in the history of UNC. Jordan was already a terrific player by the end of his freshman year due to the combination of his natural abilities and his relentless effort. Not only did Jordan's dedication astound Coach Williams, but his tremendous desire to improve his game and become an even greater player throughout his career left a big impression on Coach Williams. That never-ending thriving got Jordan his selection by the Chicago Bulls in the 1984 NBA Draft, and he later became the most successful and prominent basketball player worldwide.

"There's no way around hard work.
Embrace it."

-ROGER FEDERER

Another famous athlete known for his grace and sophistication on the tennis court is Roger Federer. He was born with talent, yet always worked to improve his skills. Similar to Michael Jordan, his persistence and endless effort over the years earned him the status of being one of the best players in the history of the game. During one of Roger Federer's interviews, he stated, "When you do something best in life, you don't really want to give that up, and for me, it's tennis." Even though he held the record for the most Grand Slam titles, a total of twenty until 2018, he continues to train to sharpen his talent.

Do not fall into the trap of believing that you will inevitably be successful if you are talented. Remember, there are people with talent like yourself, and they will surpass you if you choose to stagnate. Therefore, always try to improve as Federer did. In 2017, he developed a more aggressive style, which was especially noticeable in his return of serve. Commentators even coined the term SABR, which stood for "Sneak Attack by Roger," to describe his unconventional approach to returning serves. Instead of hitting his trademark backhand slice stroke, he began hitting more single-handed backhand shots. Federer was noticeably more perceptive and had an improved killer instinct. Due to improvements he made to his game, he was ultimately victorious in both the Australian Open and Wimbledon in 2017. In January 2018, he successfully defended his title from the previous year's Australian Open.

Federer has shown, once again, that he can win championships by diligently working to improve his natural talent. The ability to hone his superb techniques and grow as a tennis player has allowed Roger Federer to build a successful career. While competing at the highest level, he believed he was a quick learner, which in turn aided him in developing his abilities quickly: *"One of my big, big strengths I think early on in my career was that I could learn very quickly. You wouldn't have to tell me the things 10 times or 50 times until I understood them. You would only have to tell me two or three times."* Federer has established himself as one of the most successful sportsmen in the world because of his extraordinary skill, prolificacy, and work ethic. He is a perfect example of how to capitalize on strengths and turn them into a successful career.

Putting Your Gifts and Talents to Use

"To give anything less than your best is to sacrifice the gift."

-STEVE PREFONTAINE

You all have gifts and carry abilities. However, just like your fingerprint, it's different from one another. Therefore, you use your gifts and abilities differently. Sometimes, it takes a while to uncover your gifts, but once you find them, nourish and polish them. The more you take care of them, the more your life shines brightly.

The reasons to put your gifts to use:

➢ **Gifts Were Given to Be Shared**
You all have gifts that make you unique and valuable. These gifts are not meant to be hidden or hoarded, but to be shared with the world. By sharing, you are essentially inspiring,

helping, and making the world a better place. Additionally, as you share, you might end up discovering new talents, creating more opportunities, and establishing new connections. When I think of gifts and talents, it makes me think about the United States Patent and Trademark Office (USPTO). Besides the fact that intellectual property is being protected with a patent given by the USPTO, the inventors are sharing their innovations with us. Instead of hiding their discoveries through their gifts and talents, they choose to share them with the world and change our lives.

> **It Makes You Live a Happy Life**
Your natural abilities and skills are ultimately your strengths, which contribute to your self-assurance. Because of these abilities, you will be in a much happier state once you realize that you can get a task done efficiently. You will begin to see the world through a fresh perspective, one that is richer in both beauty and significance. Tony Robbins, a well-known motivational speaker, would give his talk at any time of the day or night, wherever it may be. His skill and aptitude are in the art of oratory. He takes pleasure in being on stage and delivering powerful speeches that have a positive impact on many people's lives. If you spend time engaging in activities at which you excel, you will not only bring happiness into your own life but also into the lives of others who might need a little more celebration of their own. According to a study titled "Investing in Strengths" conducted in 2003 by Donald O. Clifton, an American psychologist at the Gallup Inc., and James K. Harter, chief scientist for the Gallup Inc., employees who make daily use of their respective strengths are six times more likely to be interested in their work. In the same study, these individuals enhanced their health and well-being, experienced less anger and despair, had more energy to face the day, and attained a better degree of involvement with the work at hand.

➢ Leaving a Long-Lasting Impression on Others

The effect on the recipient is the same whether you choose to share your talents with others or provide them with a tangible present. As a karate teacher, I want to pass along to my students new information that I discover. I have a strong sense that it is my duty to teach the arts to as many people as possible. When it comes to my students, I don't set any restrictions on how I educate them. In exchange, they are constantly interested in acquiring new knowledge and consistently putting it into practice. Seeing how grateful my students were when I showed them new techniques brought me joy. I am fairly sure I am also leaving a long-lasting impression for my students because that was how I felt when my teacher taught me.

PART 2

GETTING PREPARED

5 Assessing the Current Situation

"If you want to know the past, look at the present. If you want to know the future, look at the present."

— BUDDHA

Finding Your Current Self

Before diving headfirst into the process of goal setting, it is important to take stock of where you are in terms of your mental and physical health, as well as your resources. If you know where to begin, planning and making choices when you embark on a new journey will be easier. The practice of meditation is one method to get started. While sitting straight up with your eyes closed, focusing on your breathing. Let go of any troublesome thoughts, your mind will enter a state of relaxation that will provide you with an unclouded view of the here and now. From that vantage point, you can reflect on activities or occurrences of the past. You may find reasons to confirm why you pursue your ambitions.

Knowing the benefits of meditation, I suggested this

technique as a daily routine to my karate students. To my surprise, some were extremely interested and agreed with this routine. We allotted twenty minutes each morning, Monday through Friday at 7:00 AM, to meditate via video conference. Not only does beginning the day with a peaceful mind and an unclouded vision assist in improving one's energy level throughout the day, but it also helps one become more motivated to achieve one's objectives expediently. Each morning, we started our day by closing our eyes, focusing on our breathing, and allowing our thoughts to roam. We visualized details of relishing moments when our goals were accomplished.

One of my long-term objectives has been to create my own public speaking business. Unfortunately, I didn't have much understanding of the profession, so I was nervous to begin. While meditating with my students, I wanted to learn about myself and dig deep to see if I was capable of this new endeavor. During meditation, I recalled the reasons that inspired me to pursue this goal. I was taken back to the most challenging period of my life, the journey to the United States with my father, including flashbacks of the dangerous sea that came so close to taking our lives. I remembered how I struggled in the refugee camps and adapted to my new life in the United States. Each occurrence appeared in my mind so vividly as if it happened only yesterday. Amazingly, just by shutting my eyes and focusing on past events, I was able to take my attention to a whole new level. Strength and determination came to me when I reflected on how I had prevailed through all that adversity. It was as if all the reservations and uncertainties that had been preventing me from moving forward had vanished. I saw my mission. I wanted to share my experiences of overcoming difficulty to help others overcome theirs through speaking. A new set of pictures took place in my mind. I saw myself giving presentations, mingling with my audiences, and having conversations with them. Even when the meditation was over and I had returned to the present with my eyes open, I could not shake the feeling that I could be an effective speaker.

It didn't take long until speaking opportunities knocked on my door. I was asked by several non-profit organizations and federal agencies to give a talk on leadership. For sure I was ecstatic that my dream came true and everything that I meditated upon was about to happen. On my first speaking engagement with a group of young adults, I spoke about the power of believing in yourself. As I was speaking, my mind was also playing the image that I had imagined during my meditative journey.

Jim Carrey is yet another prominent example of an individual who shaped his own path. During the first few years of his career, he had a challenging time finding employment in the entertainment sector. Jim started in standup comedy at several clubs in downtown Toronto in 1979. Unfortunately, his impersonations were seen as a failure at the time, and the outcome wasn't what he had envisioned. However, in 1985 he made a bold choice when he decided to write a check to himself for $10 million, dated ten years later, and kept the check in his wallet. Although it seemed to be an audacious action in 1985, he was offered $10 million to play the leading role in the movie *Dumb and Dumber* in November 1995. You can call it luck or the law of attraction, but what Jim Carrey did served as the impetus for him to make his goal come true. His good fortune was essentially the result of his diligent preparation meeting a favorable opportunity. It was certain that the prophecy would never be fulfilled if Carrey did nothing but wait at home for his luck to arrive. Yes, a call to action indeed was what he did, but his willpower ignited the flame. Whether you follow Jim Carrey's bold choice or meditate to envision your future, you need to bring out your desire and dedication toward the objectives you have set for yourself. When you finally realize how powerful your will to advance is, no obstacle can stop you.

"You can't go back and change the beginning, but you can start where you are and change the ending."

-C.S. LEWIS

Know What You Really Want

According to several studies, those who seek significance in their lives in addition to pleasure are the ones who report the highest levels of happiness. You are likely to experience greater levels of happiness when the aim extends beyond yourself. Living in a Nazi concentration camp was one of the most awful experiences in the world, yet Viktor E. Frankl managed to endure it. He was quoted as saying at one time, "Life is never made unbearable by circumstances, but only by lack of meaning and purpose." Discovering who you are and what makes you happy is, therefore, an endeavor that is intrinsically related to finding significance.

Here are some possible ways to begin:

➤ **Think about What You Want**
Knowing exactly what you want in life is not a simple task and is probably one of the most challenging activities to consider. One way to think about what you want in life is to reflect on your values, passions, and strengths. While having more money is probably high on the list of desires, I do believe we all have a higher purpose than just being rich. We live in a society where even the rich and famous are having mental breakdowns that eventually lead to suicide or addiction. Being content with oneself is the ultimate achievement. I believe that thinking about what you want is not a one-time exercise, but a continuous process of self-discovery and growth. Visualize what kind of lifestyle you want, the people you want to be surrounded by, and your impact on the world. If you can spend some time thinking and visualizing your goals and aspirations, you will know what your priority is on your path of discovery.

> ### Getting to Know Your Personal Power

Contentment in your life is possible when you take charge. You no longer participate in a cycle of negative thinking that convinces you there is something wrong with you or that the universe is conspiring against you. You will become a power player after you come to terms with the conviction that only you can control your fate. The process of discovering and being who you are requires that you first learn how to harness your inner strength.

> ### Change Your Belief by Silencing Your Inner Critic

Your worst enemy sometimes is your own belief. That little voice inside your head is preventing you from achieving goals and dreams that you have set for yourself. Until you determine specific reasons why you believe in a certain way, it will be impossible for you to modify your thoughts. Most of the time, beliefs get embedded in you for one of two reasons: negative remarks from others, or unfortunately, past incidents. Because these bad experiences took a toll on you, you may never want to confront them again. Since then, whenever comparable situations arise, avoiding them is your safety net. Well, it's time to replace negative thoughts with positive affirmations. You are different now. Change your belief to silence your inner critic. You, not your internal monologues, need to be in charge.

> ### Practice Compassion and Generosity

A quote attributed to Mahatma Gandhi, a political and religious leader, states that "The best way to find yourself is to lose yourself in the service of others." Practice generosity if you want to find your path in life and get what you want out of it. Furthermore, your self-esteem and self-worth also increases when you have a generous sense of purpose. I find that allowing myself to contribute time and money to non-profit organizations gives me a sense of fulfillment. To see even a small impact that I made, I know at least someone's life will change. When HIAS (Hebrew Immigrant Aid Society) sponsored my father and I from the refugee camp in the Philippines to come to the United States in 1982, our lives changed. In return, I want to do something to give back to the community to continue this divine practice of compassion and generosity.

6 Be Ready to Accept Feedback

"Negative feedback is just as valuable as positive feedback. Only critical feedback gives us insights on what to potentially improve. This is true in life and design."

– JACK CANFIELD

Hear What Others Have to Say

Back in college, I was a member of a Division II tennis team. Every time I was defeated in a match, not only did my coach provide me with comments, but my teammates also did. It was hard enough to swallow my loss, but hearing their criticism made the situation more intolerable for me. Not a single word reached my mind even though such remarks would have assisted me in improving my ability. When I reflect on those days, I regret that I allowed my disappointment to overwhelm me instead of appreciating and accepting their good will. Thankfully, after graduating from college and beginning work in the professional world, my perspective changed.

After a few months of boredom while working at the

engineering company that I shared in the previous chapter, I met Liam, a coworker who was a sales engineer. Thanks to his advice, I decided to transition to the engineering sales department since I believed I had some expertise in sales. Prior to working for this company, I used to sell Cutco™ cutlery by going door to door to find potential customers. Believing in my past experiences and skills in persuading clients, I was sure that it would be a smart move for me. A month passed in my new role, yet I was unable to make a single sale. After seeing how frustrated I was, Liam handed me one of the hydraulic filters and instructed me to find a way to sell it to him.

I began my presentation in the same manner that I had done with the cutlery. Holding the filter in my hand, I described its advantages. When I finished, Liam shook his head and provided unanticipated criticism. He spent more than an hour pointing out my mistakes and how I could have avoided them. While he was speaking, I realized I had surprisingly overlooked all those important aspects. As Liam pointed out my shortcomings, I felt ashamed and irritated at the same time. I was on the verge of leaving the room, just as I felt when I was in college receiving feedback from my teammates, but something prevented me from leaving. I was required to produce sales to maintain my position, and my survival depended upon this. Furthermore, I was eager to improve my personal development. The only way to proceed was to be open to receiving critical input. I refrained from making excuses and paid close attention to what Liam had to say. I renounced from acting in a narcissistic manner and instead viewed it as constructive criticism that would help me improve.

A few weeks later, I made my first sale after applying Liam's advice. I was grateful to not only surviving the job, but to see how much I had grown. From that point on, I was hungry for comments and feedback. I absorbed every single one of them, regardless of favorability. Even if the criticism did not pertain to my core competencies, at least I had opportunity to listen and choose which aspects I should focus on improving. Hearing other people call attention to your shortcomings is rarely a pleasant experience. Nevertheless, if you can suppress your ego and transform those harsh remarks into helpful words, your progression will go beyond anything you could have anticipated. Personal development leads to the greatest levels of satisfaction.

"There is a reason why you have two ears and one mouth. Listen more and talk less."

-JOHN MAXWELL

Listening more to comprehend rather than talking back to defend yourself is also another winning point, as John Maxwell, a motivational speaker, correctly stated. I was able to take in what Liam had to say about my shortcomings and improve myself due to my silence and refusal to argue. To concentrate on my development, I set aside my ego and pride. Rather than being agitated, accept the things you lack and be okay with it. In doing so, you are giving yourself an opportunity to profit from knowledge passed down from other people.

How to Take Feedback Like a Pro

It requires a lot of strength and patience to listen to criticism in a positive manner. You are aware that the quality of your work is not perfect; yet a poor rating is not acceptable. Regrettably, being criticized is unavoidable. If you are prepared to accept it, though, it may be advantageous to both your career progress and personal growth. In addition, learning to accept feedback demonstrates that you can work effectively with others and that there is space for development in your performance. This can leave a favorable impression on your superior management, on your coworkers, or your customers.

Ways for you to take suggestions or feedbacks and leverage them into your skill set:

- **Recognizing Their Good Intentions**
  No one wants to be in a situation in which someone suggests that you "could have" or "should have" done something. To safeguard one's pride, the mind will often refuse to accept anything that isn't a compliment, much less one that exposes one's defects. Nevertheless, acknowledge their good intentions before allowing yourself to get insulted. It is possible to reduce the likelihood of repeating a mistake by being willing to accept input from other people. Take a deep breath and remind yourself that the individual is helping you with your development to achieve success. Doing so will prevent you from being irritated by the situation.

- **Listen to Understand, Not to Respond**
  Stephen R. Covey said in his book *The 7 Habits of Highly Effective People* that "We don't listen to hear; we listen to respond." He indicated that most discussions are monologues, and that people only pay attention to aspects that resonate with their core beliefs, rather than the actual substance of what is being said. I feel that when it's time to protect oneself, the individual will be constantly defending instead of listening to understand. In order to obtain value from a discussion, you must demonstrate attentiveness by actively listening to what is being said. When receiving feedback, it is important to listen thoughtfully and with interest, not to pass judgment on the other person's motivations. The most crucial thing is to not assume you are more knowledgeable than the person who is speaking.

- **Ask Questions to Understand**

  While you should try to grasp what is being said to you, you should not blindly believe everything brought to your attention. If anything is unclear, feel free to ask questions. Providing clarification on ideas demonstrates your thoughtful consideration of advice. You are interested in gaining an understanding of it so that you may use it to your benefit.

- **Be Gracious**

  Always remember to express gratitude to those who, by the input they provide, assist you in growing as a person. Thanking someone for pointing out a flaw in your performance may seem illogical, but you should do it. It is essential to show gratitude since they contributed to the development of a more improved version of you. Regardless of the motivation behind their actions, they took time to share their perspectives rather than remain silent and allow you to go down the wrong path.

- **Coming Back for More**

  Tracking your improvement over time is essential to keep improving. One comment is never enough to solve a problem. Rather, you should come back multiple times and revisit what had been missed. I have been keeping up with the World Championship of Public Speaking (WCPS) competition held annually by Toastmasters International. Before the competition, competitors, including me, would practice our presentations in a wide variety of groups. We wanted as much input as possible, whether it was from our coaches, peers, or random people. To bring a trophy home, we must first bring home many constructive comments and criticisms.

How to Utilize the Feedback to Your Strengths

---

*"Use feedback analysis to identify your strengths.
Then go to work on improving your strengths.
Identify and eliminate bad habits that hinder
the full development of your strengths. Figure
out what you should do and do it. Finally, decide
what you should not do."*

-PETER DRUCKER

Things to start implementing for your growth after receiving feedback:

- **Let It Marinate, Then Reflect**
  Denial is often the first response most people have after hearing a negative statement. Understandably, you would feel the need to defend your dignity in any situation. Your mind will generate a wide variety of explanations, leading you to feel that such criticisms are incorrect or unfair. However, allow yourself at least a couple of days to reflect. After giving yourself time to process the information, go back and look at the feedback to see if it addresses any gaps in your knowledge. When you keep your emotions under check, you will have better judgment.

- **Determine that Adjustments Need to Be Made**
  As soon as you acknowledge that you have these flaws, you can prepare to make changes. You can adjust and not be confined to a fixed position by the thoughts in your mind. You will reach a point where you can advance another notch.

- **Move Forward with an Action Plan**
  After digesting criticism and recognizing your shortcomings, it is time to devise a strategy and put it into action. To get started, consider the comments you received and make a list of the items that need to be improved. As you move toward your objective, it is motivating to look at your list and realize you have crossed off completed items.

7 Build Momentum by Doing Little Things

"It's not the big things that add up in the end; it's the hundreds, thousands, or millions of little things that separate the ordinary from the extraordinary."

– DARREN HARDY

Do Little Things for Big Results

The guiding philosophy of my karate instructor was "If you can't do little things, don't expect big results." This adage profoundly influenced the course of my life. The first time I joined sensei's class because of a flyer that read, "Free Karate" followed by "Build Your Confidence," I was immediately drawn to it. What could be better than acquiring basic self-defense skills and improving my self-assurance at the same time...for free? As a novice, I was excited, and the moment sensei stepped in, he remarked, "We will start with easy stuff." That was music to my ears. Sensei instructed the whole class to punch and kick from a half-knee bend position, which he called a "horse stance." I was happy thinking his order was indeed easy since I had practiced karate years earlier. However, thirty minutes into the class, my body wore down after those countless drills. I started to doubt what the word "easy" meant to sensei. Instead of teaching karate, he instructed us to punch and kick repetitiously. Why was he doing that? What kind of self-assurance would I get from doing this? While still confounded by sensei's intention, he put the last nail to the drill. "We have a few hundred more to go before reaching one thousand," sensei said.

I looked at sensei, wondering if he was out of his mind. Then he continued, "In order to be strong and confident, first and foremost, we need to do the easy stuff innumerably." That was when I understood persistence by building strength and stamina. If you can do the "easy stuff," you are ready when faced with more difficult challenges.

_____

*"I fear not the man who has practiced
10,000 kicks once, but I fear the
man who has practiced one kick 10,000
times."*

-BRUCE LEE

_____

Your skill may be sharpened by engaging in the activity consistently. After just a few attempts, you should not let yourself get bored or start believing that you already have it mastered. There are certain things for which you need countless hours of practice to reach your full potential; the more work you put in, the more improvement you'll see. During the years that I spent practicing karate with sensei, I picked up this valuable lesson. It was of immense assistance to me in achieving success in this artistic endeavor, as well as in other areas, including my academics. During my time at college, I consistently put this idea into practice. I spent the same amount of time practicing each of my tasks as I did with practicing my punches and kicks. Not only did I develop my discipline by doing these tedious activities, but they also helped me keep my momentum, which is almost as vital.

How to Create Momentum

---

*"Don't watch the clock, do what
it does and keep going!"*

-ANONYMOUS

Imagine pushing a shopping cart stacked high with cases of water bottles. It is always challenging to make the initial push. You need to get into a correct posture, which involves bending your knees, lowering your back, and extending your arms. Parts of your entire body will automatically work together to provide the power necessary to begin the push. As soon as those wheels on the cart begin to turn, momentum will begin to build, and all you need to do is direct the cart in the desired direction. In other words, momentum can only be started after a significant amount of initial effort has been expended. The same concept applies to gaining momentum in life. Put yourself in the best possible position by getting rid of things that drag you down. There is no need to carry negative thoughts or doubts as you embark on your journey. Immerse yourself in the task and visualize achieving the goal. By doing this, you are fueling your motivation and generating momentum. When you get the ball rolling, you can direct your desire toward whatever objective you choose, and nothing will be able to stop you.

Ways to create momentum:

- **Mind Mapping and Making Your Dream a Reality**
  What you take in visually and allow yourself to imagine can assist you in internalizing and bringing something into existence. Creating a mind map is an excellent approach to getting started. Write your ideas or thoughts on paper, as opposed to merely stating them out loud or thinking of them.

You will get a feeling of orientation. You will become aware of the course of action to pursue and the outcomes to anticipate. If you can clearly see yourself succeeding, you will make progress toward your objective far more quickly.

- **Start with The Law of Attraction**
  After creating a mental map, the next step is to put the law of attraction into practice. Maintain a consistent focus on materializing the concepts and ideas that you recorded in your mind mapping. While you are releasing your positive energy into the ether, the cosmic law is working to align your thoughts with the physical world. Although the law of attraction makes it possible for you to easily attract what you desire, you still must put in significant work if you want it to materialize. If you only make a wish, then nothing will happen, no matter how many thoughts or ideas you send out into the cosmos. It is necessary to devote your attention and effort to anything that you want to manifest.

- **Think Big and Choose Big**
  Doubting your capabilities is often one of the reasons your dreams fall short. Failure and disappointment are detrimental, and they can stop you from going forward. However, be bold and step outside of your fear to think and choose big because what is there to lose when you never had it in the first place? On the contrary, if you make it, it's not only rewarding but the feeling of accomplishment will be multiplied tenfold. If your dreams are too easy to achieve, they're not dreams, but only routine. There was a study conducted at Harvard University to evaluate people with concrete goals on how much money they wanted to make. There were only 3% that wrote down their goals. Ten years later, that 3% were making more money than the other 97% combined.

"If you rest, you'll rust!
If you recline, you decline!
If you sit, you quit!
So, get moving today!"

-DENISE AUSTIN

- **Motivation is In the Motion**
  Constantly telling yourself that you will be "getting around to" your task is a form of procrastination that we all know nothing will get done timely. It is time to quit telling that to yourself repeatedly. Waiting for inspiration to occur is the same as saying, "I don't want to do it!" However, it is possible to will oneself to be motivated. When you set anything into motion, only your action causes it to take place. When I was teaching my karate class, there were times when I observed my students lacking in strength and vitality. Instead of yelling to get them to show energy, I urged them to just keep going. On a particular day, I wasn't concerned with whether they were striking or kicking in the right manner. It wasn't the technique that I was concentrating on as much as the motion itself. Keep in mind that momentum is what drives motivation. When the body is in motion, it creates impetus, ultimately providing the urge to keep traveling in the same direction. The first thing I did was tell them to keep moving to loosen their joints. Once the body is loose, motion is created, thus momentum carried them for an hour of practice. Similarly, at work, it usually takes some time to settle at your desk before starting a project, but once you do, sometimes you don't even want to take a break.

Once It's Going, Keep It Rolling

"The most powerful ingredient in business is positive momentum. Get it and keep it!"

-UNKNOWN

As you can see, significant hard work, discipline, and dedication create that force for the initial move. Therefore, don't waste all that effort by stopping short of your dreams. When facing obstacles, take a step back, gather a new plan, and execute full mode again.

Ways to keep the momentum going:

- **Sorting Your Priority**
  The primary factor that leads you in the wrong direction is distractions. Regardless of what kind of distractions you are dealing with, determining your priorities is what will keep you going forward. You must allot a certain amount of time to each activity. Otherwise, choosing to work on unimportant things will hinder your momentum, causing you to slow down or even come to a complete stop.

- **Commit to Your Dreams**
  If you are not committed to making your dreams come true, they are at risk of being lost. The first step in building momentum is committing to do actions that are in line with your goals. There may be times when you have a sense of disorientation and turn away. Reflect on your subconscious to figure out why you are having this dream in the first place. As soon as you discover it, your degree of dedication will reignite.

- **Celebrate the Small Wins**

For either big or small dreams, achievement takes time and effort. Therefore, they each deserve a celebration, even if it is a small or insignificant one. Celebrations are mile markers telling you the journey to your goal is near, just like in driving, mile markers on the roadside signal your destination is closer. When you permit yourself to celebrate these seemingly little victories, you generate enthusiasm that motivates you to continue, which in turn keeps the momentum going.

8 Practice Propagates Progress

"The formula for success is simple: Practice and concentration then more practice and more concentration."

—MILDRED ELLA (BABE) DIDRIKSON ZAHARIAS

Progress Not Perfection

After putting in countless hours of practice, one's ultimate objective should be to achieve perfection. Is there any truth to this assertion? Is the final objective to reach perfection after dedicating countless hours, suffering through agony, and standing up after each failure? Where do we find perfection? The truth is, there is no correct response.

When watching gymnasts perform at the Olympics, I thought they were flawless. Based on my opinion, it was a foregone conclusion that they would get the highest score possible from the judges. However, when their scores were shown, I was astonished that only a few were deemed as masterly. The reality is that various people have differing conceptions of what constitutes perfection. I think that perfection is subjective, existing only in the eyes of the observer.

It is good discipline to strive towards excellence. Sadly, since it is an abstraction, there is no method to quantify it. When I was in college, my good buddy, Tom, worked on a project in which he had to construct a prosthetic hand. Tom devoted numerous hours to the investigation and development of what he referred to as "a perfect hand." He went out of his way to ensure that the hand was operating properly, paying attention to even the smallest details. We did not doubt that Tom would place in the top spot. Surprisingly, the winner was someone else in the class. We believed Tom's hand was superior and faultless. However, it did not appear that way to the judges. This demonstrated that there was more than one method to challenge perfection. Everyone who sits in judgment, including those judges, you, and me, do it in our unique manner.

Having realized that perfection is in the eye of the beholder, should you now stop giving your best attempt? Well, that is not the case either. You should constantly provide your utmost effort in whatever you're working on. The key distinction is rather than focusing on perfecting something, you should consider how far you have improved. In other words, the method of perfecting such talents needs to be modified so that it emphasizes growth rather than completion. It will be far more satisfying to recognize your improvement each day than it would be to perfect yourself.

How striving for perfection can hinder you in the process:

- **"If I can't do it perfectly then what's the point of keep continuing?"**
  Three years ago, I embarked on a new challenge, writing my first novel, *Split Up by the Sea*. This book is a chronicle of my journey to the United States with my father in search of freedom after the fall of Saigon in 1975. I wanted to dedicate this book to my family, as well as to all the people who escaped by boat and endured the same struggles that my

father and I had when we immigrated. Over countless nights of losing sleep and making pots of coffee, I aimed to write this memoir as good as it could be. I desired for my memoir to be on par with other writers. Stressfully, the more I wrote, the more I ended up erasing since I wasn't satisfied with what I created. The impression that it couldn't be as good as other writers made me want to give up. Fortunately, receiving an encouraging comment from my wife, "I think your book is good," inspired me to continue writing. Oftentimes, you constantly hold yourself to an unreasonable standard, which ends up causing you more harm than good. There are times when all you need to do is take stock of how far you've come and be proud of it. I was glad that I didn't stop writing and instead, listened to my wife's encouragement to continue. It was a daunting process, but I was able to publish the book in November 2022, in time to mark the 40th anniversary of my father and me immigrating to the United States. Additionally, my book was on Amazon's best seller list the day it debuted and won the Best Indie Choice award for nonfiction a few months later.

- **It Diminishes Self-confidence if continuing to be Self-critical.**
  Being meticulous may lower self-esteem by fostering doubt. While striving to be a perfectionist, you are establishing unattainable objectives and judging yourself harshly, resulting in a cycle of failure and self-criticism. Therefore, you will reinforce feelings that you are not good enough. Get rid of self-criticism and doubt to prevent perfectionism's detrimental consequences on confidence. Accept that errors and failure are normal, and exactness is impossible. Instead, allow yourself to celebrate your gains and learn from your setbacks.

- **It Deprives You of the Present Moment**
  Being a perfectionist might cause you to live in a state of perpetual worry and anxiety due to your preoccupation with

the future. When you strive for perfection, you often overlook the present in favor of planning for the future. This results in a disconnection from people in your immediate environment and your inability to enjoy the splendors of the moment. You may get caught up in trying to be flawless that you forget to relax and appreciate life as it is now. This may lead to exhaustion and a loss of meaning in life. Mindfulness and living in the present are crucial for perfectionists who struggle with this propensity. Enjoy the moment and live for the moment! Appreciate yourself, as each of you has unique qualities and characteristics to shine distinctively.

- **You Might End Up Isolating Yourself from People**
  Some individuals may believe your standard is too high for them, and as a result, they will have an incorrect impression of you. Even if you believe that you do not exhibit arrogance, the fact that you are always attempting to prove that you are an ideal person creates an environment in which other people do not feel comfortable being around you.

Aim to Be Better Than Your Best!

"Don't strive to be better than others; strive to be better than your best self."

-ANONYMOUS

One of my favorite activities in my late teenage years was playing tennis. However, because my family was on a tight budget, my father was unable to provide me with any tennis instruction or even the means to purchase a racket. I didn't have an opportunity to get one until I was in high school. It took me a considerable amount of effort to persuade my father to give me the money to purchase a used one from my friend, Ben. I couldn't contain my joy when I realized that I could finally participate in the sport. Only one snag: I didn't know how to play tennis. Since I didn't want to give up, I resolved to teach myself. My first tennis lesson began at a handball court, which consisted of a concrete wall with an enclosed fence in a park in New York City. Ben had given me some old balls to get started. I didn't get any decent instruction, so I ended up wielding the racket like a hammer and smashing the ball all over the place rather than into the wall. The ultimate result was that I spent more time picking up balls than I did hitting them. One day, a guy who happened to be walking by saw my absurd hitting. He urged me to wait and then returned with a book authored by Arthur Ashe, one of the greatest tennis players of all time. Inside, Ashe demonstrated all the fundamental techniques that a novice like me would need to know. Even though the book helped teach me with the correct strokes and serves, I still felt like I needed more, namely a professional coach.

Since Ben was aware that my ambition was to play for the school's tennis team, he connected me with his coach, Mr. Tanenbaum, whom we called "Coach T." He offered a free tennis clinic for children at the National Tennis Center (NTC), which is also the location of the U.S. Open. I couldn't express how happy I was to have a coach at last. Although my commute required me to catch a train at five in the morning, I was delighted to have the opportunity to advance personally.

I never missed a single class with Coach T, not even when the weather was bad. Even when other children soundly defeated me on the court, I carefully continued to practice, refusing to give up because I was thankful I could acquire this knowledge at no cost. I had faith that if I persisted, my skills would eventually get better. I wasn't aiming for perfection; rather, I was aiming for the improvement of my skills. After diligently training every day for three months, I was selected for the team.

My commitment to always be better never changed. I continually worked hard on the practice court with my teammates and put all effort into chasing after every ball during my matches.

For the next two years playing for my high school tennis team, I was always on the roster to play the top four. During my senior year, we won our area and headed for the Division Championship. On the day of our finals, coach T was present and watched our matches. During the changeover, he stood by the fence and screamed, "You are at your best right now." At that moment, the only thing I could think of was playing my best instead of the trophy. Because I was focusing on my improvements, I played my heart out. As for the outcome, I won my match and our school brought home the Division Championship.

I started as a disadvantaged kid who couldn't afford a racket, but I've worked hard to become a better version of myself. The fulfillment of my ambition did not end there; I was invited to join a collegiate tennis team in Division II. To this day, whenever I step foot on the court, my primary objective is not to become a great player, but rather to perform to the highest level of my capability.

Benefits of Practice for Progress Instead of Perfection

"The primary benefit of practicing any art, whether well or badly, is that it enables one's soul to grow."

-KURT VONNEGUT JR.

The key to being satisfied and attaining inner peace while concentrating on one goal at a time and improving oneself, is to engage in regular practice. You should practice being in the now rather than dwelling on errors of the past or worrying about what could happen in the future. When you are aware of and acknowledge your present level of expertise, you will be better equipped to find delight in the process of improving your performance.

Benefits when you value progression instead of perfection:

> **Having Less Stress**
> When you aim for progression, you are setting realistic and achievable goals, which ultimately make you happy during the process. Rather than being too critical of yourself, you are more compassionate towards your flaws. After a year as a sales engineer, I was given an opportunity to lead the Northeast region, which consisted of New York, New Jersey, Massachusetts, and Connecticut, by introducing our hydraulic filtration system to companies and power plants. I wanted to impress my boss and worked hard. Each quarter, I was rated for how many companies bought our products and used our services. In the first quarter, I was ten percent above quota. However, during the second quarter, finding new customers was much tougher. I lost many nights of sleep and worked long hours to find clients, but near the end of the second quarter, I missed quota by five percent. I realized that being new at this position, I was too excited, set unrealistic goals, and ended up causing myself stress. Instead of trying to overachieve as a novice, I should have aimed to meet the expected goal, then later go for the bigger goal as I gained more experience.

> **Elevating Your Skill Level**
> One satisfying feeling is to achieve goals that you've set. Whether you are learning a new language, mastering a musical instrument, or excelling at your job, it can only be accomplished if you agree to put in the time and effort to develop these skills. The benefits of taking your skill to another level will give you a sense of happiness and fulfillment that comes from within. Self-satisfaction is important to your well-being, as it boosts your self-esteem, confidence, and motivation. You are not settling for mediocrity or complacency but striving for excellence and mastery. You are opening yourself to opportunities and experiences that can enrich your life. You are also contributing to the world with your unique talents and

abilities. I've never met anyone who engaged in regular practice and did not have positive outcomes.

> **Creating New Habits**

Habits are the routines and behaviors that you repeat regularly and unconsciously. They can be both positive and negative, depending on whether they help you or hinder you in achieving your goals or daily living. I believe that when you develop new habits, you accept to replace bad ones so that you can improve your life. For example, creating a habit of exercising regularly can improve your health. Creating a habit of not eating late (after 7 PM) would improve sleeping. Creating a habit of gratitude can certainly help you become happier and appreciate the things that you currently have. The most important thing about creating new habits is that you challenge yourself to step out of your comfort zone and try new things.

> **Building Your Confidence Level**

Another advantage of tracking your advancement is boosting your self-confidence. At each new degree of progress, you should feel proud of the devoted hours and laborious work you put in to achieving the previous level. Enjoy the satisfaction of the effort that you dedicated during those months, weeks, or days. I believe that tennis, especially in a singles match, allows you to acquire self-confidence quickly. If you don't grasp self-confidence, it isn't your opponent that beats you, but instead, you beat yourself. Throughout my years of playing tennis, both competitively in college and as a recreational player, the game forces me to make an independent decision quickly and with conviction. There is only yourself on the court that is cheering you on. Therefore, to build your confidence is to continually practice. Wherever your stage of expertise is, be confident at that level. If you are an intermediate player, be confident facing other intermediate competitors.

PART 3

R.I.S.E. AND TAKE ACTION

9 Create Your Action Plan

"A dream written down with a date becomes a goal. A goal broken down into steps becomes a plan. A plan backed by action makes your dreams come true."

–GREG S. REID

It Begins with a Plan

---

*"We succumb to fear
because our plan is not clear!"*

-LEN TRAN

Regardless of what you aim to do in life, from trivial to significant goals, a thorough plan is what you need to start. A plan will help minimize the chance of failure or defeat. Have you heard of a 'SMART' goal? Applying SMART goals will get you to where you want to be.

Here is a breakdown of a SMART goal:

-   **S**pecific
-   **M**easurable
-   **A**chievable
-   **R**ealistic
-   **T**imely

These key points will help make your goals clearer and easier to follow.

-   **S**pecifying your goals by clearly stating the desired outcome and expectations.
-   **M**easure your progress and personal development numerically to define your goal and track your progress.
-   **A**chieving what you are tasked to do with confidence given your current available resources.
-   **R**ealistic or relevant goals mean you get satisfaction when you keep getting good results.
-   **T**imeliness will help you complete your goals by the desired due date.

Apply These Questions to Your SMART Goals

➢ **Specific**
-   What exactly am I looking to accomplish?
-   Who are the team members to get me there?
-   How am I going to accomplish it?

➢ **Measurable**
-   What is my target number (quantity or percentage)?
-   Do I measure every small win or only the big ones?

➢ **Achievable**
-   What do I need to achieve this goal?
-   If I don't have what I need, how do I get it?

- ➢ **Realistic**
  - Why am I setting this goal?
  - Would this goal help my current situation (Business, Personal)?
  - Is this goal aligned with my mission and value?

- ➢ **Timely**
  - Can I reach this goal by a certain date?
  - If not, what is the next reasonable date?
  - When is the hard deadline?

Putting It All Together

"Planning is bringing the future into the present so that you can do something about it now."

-ALAN LAKEIN

Now you have a precise plan in place. You also understand your "why" and how to find your purpose to move forward. It is time to execute. However, what happens if somewhere during the process, your purpose seems disoriented and your enthusiasm diminished? I am sure you are familiar with *New Year's Resolutions*. Goals were established and vows were made. Nevertheless, most of these resolutions died during the first month or two. The reason: It was not that the objectives were particularly challenging; rather, motivation to keep going dwindled, and quitting was probably going to result. Don't fret, this is when my **R.I.S.E.** comes into play to save the day. You must be curious as to why it is spelled *R.I.S.E.* and not *rise*. There is no doubt that the meaning and pronunciation are identical. Albeit a more profound understanding of it is what I want to impart to you. Throughout my life, I've learned that to ensure a path to your final goal (success), you need a system other than a thorough plan and knowing your "why."

I believe fear is the primary reason individuals fail to achieve their goals. Fear acts as a barrier that prevents people from taking risks. Often, we succumb to fear because our plans lack clarity.

In April 2023, I received an invitation to deliver a TEDx talk in Woodbridge, Virginia. Initially, I instinctively said yes, but simultaneously, I felt an immediate surge of nervousness. I had spoken on many platforms, but a TEDx stage of more than 38 million subscribers on YouTube™ made me feel as though my subject would not be viewed by many. As I contemplated the topic to address, the TEDx organizer wanted me to talk about overcoming fear, which was within my subject matter expertise. However, there are countless talks about fear on YouTube™. How could I make mine different to catch the viewers' interest?

It was then I decided to share with the world my **R.I.S.E.** system, a system with a well-defined plan to help people overcome their fears. Just like how engineers come up with formulas to solve equations, I believe that our minds can be engineered for success as well. As in previous chapters, I mentioned that our minds conjured negative thoughts to disrupt our path to success. This **R.I.S.E.** system is the recipe for relinquishing your fear.

I strongly believe that our lives can be likened to maps. Just as we require a map to navigate from point A to point B, we must also map out our life's journey. Without a map, following directions from someone would naturally create anxiety. However, if provided with a detailed map that outlines every twist and turn, we would be better prepared. The same principle applies to our lives. To confidently pursue our goals, we need our personal map—the **R.I.S.E.** system. Understanding the essence of **R.I.S.E.**, which stands for "**Recognize, Initialize, Strategize, and Energize,**" has been instrumental in my journey. In the next four chapters, I will elaborate on each one of them and how it will help you create your plan.

As you read through the next four chapters, I recommend

you also grab a pen and paper, or any writing means, to jot down the goals that you had failed or any goal that you are having now. As you follow along with the **R.I.S.E.** system, you will learn something about yourself that you might not have known before. I believe that having written words appear in front of you is a way for you to see things clearer. People tend to take action when written goals appear in front of them.

10 Let's Recognize

"I hated every minute of training, but I said... Don't quit. Suffer now and live the rest of your life as a champion."

–MUHAMMAD ALI

R.I.S.E. - Recognize

The first **R** in **R.I.S.E.** is **Recognize to revitalize.** You must first acknowledge the circumstances in which you find yourself at this very moment. Are you taking any steps toward achieving your objectives? Do you feel that you are unable to continue because you do not know how or where to begin? Are you lacking enthusiasm because you've been unsuccessful in the past?

The primary factor that contributes to the failure of objectives is a lack of excitement throughout the process. There is a wide range of possible explanations for this. However, the fundamental problem is lack of drive.

The following are common reasons why people lose motivation:

➤ Being Burned Out

A condition known as "burnout" is a severe kind of tiredness that is brought on by an ongoing sense of being overwhelmed. It happens when you feel unable to satisfy incessant demands placed on you and are overwhelmed by your emotions. You start to lose interest in certain functions as well as the drive that drove you to pursue that role initially. As stress persists, it will ultimately influence other aspects of your life, such as your professional life, your personal life, and your social life. When this happens, your body is more likely to become susceptible to disease which may ultimately cause you to give up.

➤ Having Doubts About Yourself

Self-doubt is doubting oneself and one's ability. When confronting obstacles, making choices, or pursuing objectives, self-doubt is a common human feeling. Self-doubt may lead to negative thinking, fear of failure, and comparing oneself to others. It may prevent you from taking chances, seizing opportunities, and reaching your full potential.

➤ Being in the Wrong Crowd

Being part of the wrong crowd may be detrimental to your personal growth. When you surround yourself with people who do not encourage you to pursue your objectives or provide growth opportunities, you risk being satisfied and stuck in a rut. It is possible that because of this, you may be less likely to seek out new experiences, learn from a variety of views, or challenge yourself to go beyond your limit—all of which are necessary for individual development and success.

➤ Being Impatient

Impatience may prevent you from being successful in many ways, but one of those ways is by causing you to have excessively lofty expectations. When you lack patience, you may establish objectives that are unreasonably difficult or anticipate quick results without considering the amount of time and work necessary to achieve such goals. This may lead to disappointment, frustration, and a feeling of failure when you do not see instant improvement. Certainly, after seeing that you are not moving at a desired pace, you can be demoralized and impeded to work toward your objectives. In 2010 when I built my basement, I was excited to get the job rolling and scheduled an estimated date to finish. It didn't take long until I faced my first frustration. Installing the supporting beams from the concrete floor was daunting. I didn't realize the amount of labor involved, including measuring, carrying, nailing, sawing, and many more. After about forty two-by-four studs were assembled, I was running out of patience; my measurements weren't exact and nailing were off-center. When I took a break and moved a few feet back, I noticed that the structure was not properly aligned. If I were to put drywall sheets onto the studs, I realized that the wall wouldn't be straight if I continued. Being impatient caused me to disassemble a portion of the structure. After removing most of the studs, I was unmotivated to start again. Although I managed to redo the framing work, it was a valuable lesson to be patient.

➢ Unattainable Objectives
Unrealistic goals normally end up with unachievable results. A common factor that contributes to unachievable results is that your objectives are not based on reality. When you create objectives that are unattainable or too idealistic, most likely you won't have a grasp on resources, talents, and/or time needed to reach such goals. Once you are unable to make meaningful progress toward these objectives, feelings of frustration, discouragement, and a sense of failure are expected outcomes.

Now after **recognizing** why you've lost motivation; it is time to get back on track. What you need to do is get back your enthusiasm. In other words, you need to **revitalize**.

How Do We Revitalize?

➢ **Focus on Your "Why"**
Think back to when you chose to pursue this objective or complete this endeavor. What exactly was it about the objective that excited you so much? In what ways did you see yourself ultimately becoming successful? Which "why" were you referring to? Once you have answers to all these questions, elaborate on the reasons driving you as well as the benefits that will result. Proceed in this manner until you experience that sensation of excitement again. When I started my karate school teaching students for free, I constantly asked myself, "Why am I doing this?" I already had a job, and I certainly did not need to do this because it took time away from my family and work. By asking the "why" repeatedly, each time I came up with an answer. I finally solidified my reasons for teaching. It wasn't only for the pleasure of teaching karate, but more of fulfilling my passion to help people appreciate how much they can do with their bodies.

➢ **Ask Yourself What Would Happen If You Stopped Now**
Would you be feeling defeated and depressed if you stopped? How many people would you let down? Is this really your character?

Years ago, I met a friend, Sensei Ralph Sanchez, a 6th-degree black belt, who has been training and teaching Shorin-Ryu karate for more than forty years. He was in his mid-sixties with an injured shoulder, worn cartilage on both knees, and a tight back. As we practiced, he said, "Len, I used to be fast and strong, but now my body is not allowing me to do all those techniques anymore."

I looked at him and said, "But you have more knowledge now than before." My biggest fear was hearing from a karate friend that he would no longer practice and retire from karate.

Instead, he said, "Even if I can't move like I used to, I can't quit. My students are important to me and they need me to keep the fire burning." Upon hearing how he treasured his students, I felt an immediate connection with him. He and I had the same thinking that as leaders, we just couldn't abandon our followers.

> **Look at How Far You Have Gone**
I am sure during your journey toward your goal, you struggled with some obstacles. You may have overcome certain obstacles and kept on going, but other times, some obstacles made you throw in the towel. If you have gone far in your quest, don't throw away your hard work because you can't endure the challenge. Allow the challenge that you are encountering to give you strength. Don't run away from it but find a way to improve yourself. You will be surprised at how capable you are once you have enough information to accept the challenge.

> **Change Your Perception, Change Your Reality**
Instead of seeing an obstacle appearing in front of you, visualize it as a stepping stone to your dream. The road to success is never easy but is filled with obstacles and hindrances. However, after changing your perception, these obstacles are just your stopping point to rest and reenergize, so you can move forward again.

> **Appreciate the Learning Lesson Along the Way**
The act of learning is a step in the process of maturing. As you make progress toward your objective, you open yourself to new experiences and pick up instructive lessons along the way. Keep in mind that none of those teaching moments were bestowed upon you for no reason; rather, they were earned by the virtue of your doggedness and perseverance. Therefore, you may consider these lessons priceless treasures you can keep for the rest of your life.

Recognize What's Wrong and Move Along

When confronted with an unanticipated obstacle, you shouldn't immerse yourself in the problem that caused it. Investigate several options that might help you get out of your situation. The experience I gained from playing tennis has prepared me to do this. It makes no difference how precisely I control the balls while I'm practicing on the tennis court. When playing an actual match, hitting the ball is completely different compared to the practice sessions. The physical component is still there, but the cerebral component suffered due to my inability to read my opponent. I must take prompt action if I sense that I am about to lose control. There is not enough time to spend condemning myself for making mistakes; rather, I should focus on what I have done well in the past. If I want to have a shot at winning the match, I must make some adjustments.

It is inevitable that no matter how much planning and preparation goes into achieving a goal, there will be mishaps and setbacks along the journey. When this occurs, you shouldn't concentrate on what you did wrong; instead, own your errors, make necessary adjustments, and proceed with a more resilient attitude and a double down on your commitment to achieve the objective.

"Since everything is a reflection of our minds, everything can be transformed by our minds."

-GONG QIN

---

11 Let's Initialize

"How to begin the journey? You need only to take the first step. When? There is always now."

-GEORGE LEONARD

R.I.S.E. - Initialize

The **I** in **R.I.S.E.** stands for **Initialize to materialize**. You set your goal, plan it well, and the ultimate step is to act on it. However, uncertainty and reluctance begin to set in. It gives you the impression that you are not in the best possible condition to take the first move. You are unable to go ahead because you do not trust yourself and your situation. This is the point when plans are delayed, and finally, they either vanish into thin air or become impossible to carry out. Take for instance the case of my daughter, Lara. She has a naturally lovely voice as I had mentioned earlier. She contemplated starting a singing channel on YouTube™ for as long as she could remember. To show my support, I bought her a professional camera. She mentioned that the lighting in her room seemed too dark, so I purchased spotlights. After she was provided with the lighting that she requested, there was still no sign of filming. This time around, the quality of the sound was not satisfactory. Once again, I upgraded her microphone. In the end, despite having access to all the necessary equipment, there was still no recording.

What do you think caused her to delay or postpone her plan? When I looked at the camera sitting on her desk, as well as the two spotlights and microphone that were gathering dust, I knew it wasn't procrastination. It was her anxiety and trepidation about making that first move that caused the delay. She devised a variety of pretexts to persuade me to purchase the aforementioned items, under the assumption that doing so would facilitate the creation of an ideal setting to assist her in preparation. The fact is that she could have begun at any moment without that upgraded equipment. It was her uncertainty and reluctance that prevented her from making that first move.

Tony Robbins was quoted as saying, "Motion is what creates emotion." Whatever you're experiencing at this very moment is directly tied to the way that you're utilizing your body. I didn't want my daughter to fail at achieving her goal. I asked her to help me set up the camera, the microphone, and the lighting. While arranging the equipment, I led the conversation as to how she always had a passion for singing, even when she was a little child. I reminded her of the time she earned high praise following her performance at a birthday celebration, demonstrating how courageous she was to perform. During our conversation, I had a glimpse of the fire in her eyes that had been reignited in pursuit of her objective. She exuded the impression that she was enthusiastic and couldn't wait for the action to begin. As soon as we finished setting up the equipment, she took out her guitar, switched on the light, turned on the camera, and started filming. She completed her first song in one take. I was pleased how it turned out. Was it a flawless video that she made? From my viewpoint, it wasn't. Despite this, she took the initiative to take that initial step to conquer her shyness. She accomplished it rather than giving up on her objective before she had even begun working toward it. Don't overthink things; just get it done. There is no such thing as a perfect moment, yet only you can convert any moment into a perfect one. My daughter launched herself forward by taking that first step, which generated momentum for her. After that, several of her songs were uploaded to her channel.

What causes a lack of initiative?

> **Doubt or Lack of Confidence**
> As an adult, you often find yourself thinking and analyzing, then thinking and analyzing once again when encountering any situation. While going through this phase, your mind will be filled with random thoughts, including spurring negative thoughts over positive ones. Soon, these negative thoughts will take over unknowingly. In other words, the more you ponder, the more doubt and destructive thoughts enter your mind, making you feel insignificant and convincing you that quitting is the most prudent course of action. This is a point at which your hopes and ambitions are cut short before they've even begun. A plan that is not carried out is, in the end, nothing more than a fantasy that will at some point be forgotten.

> **Seeking For Perfectionism**
> You are seeking approval, striving for the best outcome, and wanting certainty. These are the primary motivations that drive individuals to strive for excellence. Sadly, these are also the things that prevent you from progressing. If you are too busy to demonstrate your value, then you may miss out on some fantastic possibilities. As I mentioned in the previous chapter about perfectionism, striving for perfection is not a wise thing to do in every situation. You need to have judgment to know when to give up and when to continue. Pursuing anything aimlessly often results in more problems than it solves.

> **Goal Setting Was Abstract**
> If you are not dedicated to or involved in achieving a goal, there is good probability that your goal was clouded with ambiguity. Your goal might be a hurried choice brought on by the pressure of others, or it could just be a means to pass the time. As a result, about ninety-nine percent of attempts

to achieve such objectives are likely to be fruitless. Why does this occur? Sometimes you want to fit in or have the fear of missing out (FOMO). After working for a year at the United States Patent and Trademark Office (USPTO), a few of my colleagues were signing up to attend night classes to get their law degrees. Seeing that getting a law degree could help with my career, I immediately bought the LSAT workbook and studied. I set some time to review materials in the workbook, but on the other hand, my workload at the USPTO was constantly bombarding me. After a couple of months of preparing for the LSAT and working a full-time job, I was unable to continue with the pursuit of a law degree. I realized that my goal setting for a law degree was an act of impulse. Witnessing that my colleagues were enthusiastic to obtain a law degree made me feel as though I should do the same. However, my goal setting was different from theirs. I was more focused on concentrating to get my work at the USPTO done for promotion versus a law degree. My goal setting for the law degree was ambiguous.

> **Living an Unhealthy Lifestyle**
  Your energy level will most likely decrease by leading an unhealthy lifestyle, which includes being inactive, eating poorly, not getting enough sleep, and experiencing stress. Bear in mind that your health is an especially crucial element because of the influence it has on your daily activities. For your mind and body to work properly, you need to have a high amount of energy. On the other hand, having a low level of energy will cause you to feel exhausted, uninterested, and depressed. These feelings will ultimately triumph and cause you to lose passion in life if you let them. Therefore, making changes to your lifestyle, such as increasing the amount of exercise you get, improving the quality of the food you consume, increasing the amount of time you spend sleeping, and reducing the amount of stress you experience, can help raise your energy level.

➤ **Feeling Overwhelmed**

Taking on many plans and objectives and not being sure which one to focus on achieving first sets you up to be overwhelmed. When you think more, you increase the likelihood of feeling as if you are losing control of your life. In the end, you give up because the circumstances you've created for yourself have been too overwhelming. Therefore, if you are unable to effectively manage your time, your priorities, and your emotional state, you will find it difficult to begin the process.

To sum up, **Initializing** means you are preparing the necessary conditions and resources for your goal to become a reality. Taking that first step is crucial. Without initialization, your idea will remain just an idea and never materialize into a successful venture.

How to initialize?

➤ **Destroy the Inner Distractions**

What does it mean to be distracted? Is it lacking focus, poor relationships with negative people, constant attending to your mobile phone, too many tasks all at once, or negative ideas in your mind? Let's face reality, at least two of these have happened to you simultaneously while you tried to achieve your goal, especially the negative ideas in your mind. During my time as a Process Chemical Engineer at the Department of Environmental Protection (DEP) in New York City, I was assigned to a wastewater treatment plant. My task was to make sure the treatment tanks were meeting clean water standards before sending the treated water into the Hudson River. I was excited about having a responsible role and meaningful job. However, I worried something might go wrong, or I might miss the routine regulations constantly playing in my head. I thought if I messed up, then the entire city would be affected by polluted water. It petrified me.

My thoughts became a distraction, which led me to put in a request to transfer to a different department. During a conversation with my boss, she appreciated my concern but told me that I should trust in my ability and not let unconstructive thoughts distract me from my work. She said, "We are working as a team. Everyone here is held responsible to keep the public safe. Not just only you." She also added, "My door is always open for consultation if anything goes wrong." Hearing her affirmation, I realized it wasn't my qualification, but it was my negative ideas that played tricks on me. Sometimes, our distractions can deter us before we start.

Minimize distractions by visualizing the positives and destroying the negatives. Those destructive ideas that go through your mind have the potential to be very harmful if you do not learn to manage them. If you allow them to get out of control for a lengthy period, they will sap your energy. When you hold these kinds of beliefs in your head, future experiences will be unpleasant. You will leap to the worst conclusions, even though you haven't analyzed the circumstances to see how you may reduce the severity of the problem. Regrettably, this behavior does not provide anything of value but rather increases the likelihood of becoming a gloomy person who believes that whining is the solution to problems. In the end, this will deplete your energy, causing you to lose whatever enthusiasm or passion you had. It takes practice to manage your thoughts, and the best way is to concentrate on positive thinking.

> **Identify and Address Your Fears**
Have you ever discovered that you are better at advising others than yourself? It's not that you don't like hearing your voice; rather, the reality is that it's far simpler to say than to do. Fear and uncertainty are holding you back, even though you are aware of how to start and what is required. You wind up serving as an advisor to other people and end up being a

disappointed spectator while others carry out your plan. Let's stop all that! Now is the time to focus on yourself. It is time to pinpoint the source of your anxiety and find a solution. Train your mind to believe that your fears and concerns are nothing more than illusions. Put an end to acting like a bystander, have faith in yourself, and carry out your plan of action.

Being raised in the South Bronx of New York City as an immigrant, I never had an education comparable to that of my fellow college friends who were living in better parts of New York City. In elementary school, while other students were learning at a normal pace, I was trying to catch up by learning the English language. The school didn't have the resources to fully accommodate someone of my status. I felt as though my entire education was always playing catch up. Entering my college education, I feared that once again I would be behind. It wasn't until I met a fellow student, Andrew, in my math class that my perspective changed. Andrew was a veteran in his late forties. While he and I studied, I looked at how he struggled with certain portions of math. After I helped him figure out the solution, he said to me, "I might be slow, but I am not giving up until I get my engineering degree." After hearing what Andrew said, I thought to myself, why do I have to focus on the fear that I am behind others? Having the fear constantly replaying in my head served no purpose but to make me apprehensive each time I was placed in a group project. The fear made me doubt myself. Andrew's words helped me understand what I needed to do to address fear and that was to keep moving. When you stay still, fear finds a way to creep in and stop you from any intention to move forward. When you identify your fear, finding a solution to address it is not hard. In my case, I simply resolved my fear by doing what Andrew did and that was investing more time on subjects that I was lagging. In the end, I still graduated at the same time as my classmates, so in reality, I was not behind.

➢ **Set Your Sight on the Finish Line**
The most effective way for crossing the finish line is to make it as vivid as possible. Imagine something in your mind's eye. Even better, sketch it out and create a visual representation of it on paper, in your diary, on your phone, or any place that you can access whenever you choose. Your motivation to work toward that goal will increase in proportion to the amount of detail you put into painting that image. Your mind won't be able to determine if that picture is genuine or phony as long as you keep staring at it. As you are continuing your path, the image of being victorious should constantly be replayed. It doesn't matter what challenges you may confront, the phrase, "Face it until you make it," should be your motto until the finish line.

"Don't wait until you are ready to act. Instead, take action to be ready."

-JENSEN SIAW

Initialize and Embrace the Flow

In March 2020, due to the COVID-19 pandemic, my karate school was shut down. I can empathize with the situation, given that everyone was forced to change their routines because of the lockdown. After being forced to stay indoors for days, I decided not to wait until we received advice from the Center for Disease Control (CDC) that it was safe to reopen the school. Instead, I opened my class online by using a virtual platform to continue teaching my students. I was aware that in addition to ensuring everyone in my karate class, including myself, continued their training, we needed to support and encourage one another via the use of video recordings. Although every one of my students adjusted to the new circumstances, the vibe was quite different. Because we could only communicate with one another via the camera, there was a severe loss of both connection and motivation among us. When compared to training in person, the level of intensity and excitement was lower. Instead of trying to adapt to a slower tempo, I promptly urged my students to keep up the motion that we had been doing and continue to punch and kick while imagining that they were in the same classroom by gazing at the faces of each person on the screen. The intensity increased, and so did everyone's spirit. During breaks, we engaged in conversation and lighthearted banter in the same manner we did in the classroom. Because of that initial move, we had the momentum to keep going throughout the class, and it was all because of that first action. We were able to meet and practice together every day and make it through those stressful months thanks to technology.

It's impossible to predict how taking one step can lead to additional possibilities and interests appearing in life. As an engineer who is familiar with numbers and formulas, I never imagined in my wildest dreams I'd become an author. However, after taking that initial step to writing my first memoir, *Split Up by the Sea*, who would have guessed I'd return to write my second book, namely this book?

Overall, the reason I got this far was because of that first step to embark on this new challenge. Instead of waiting for the right opportunity to present itself, I decided to seize the situation and make it work for me. I did not wait for the drive to begin operating; rather, I moved to activate it.

> **Share It with Your Trusted People**
> Some people I know do not like to share what they do as they fear failure will make them look bad. For me, allowing my trusted friends into my plans make me feel obligated to do something. Take out the impression that your friends will laugh at you for failing. Close and trusted friends would not judge you for fumbling through your goals. Instead, they would admire your dedication and courage for taking on something. The benefit of telling your friends of your

journey is that they will be your cheering crowd and you don't want to let them down. Sharing your plan with your friends is certainly a way to help you take that first step toward your goal. It makes you feel compelled to do it. Keeping the plan to yourself may give permission to procrastinate.

12 Let's Strategize

"Strategy without tactics is the slowest route to victory. Tactics without strategy is the noise before defeat."

-SUN TZU

R.I.S.E. - Strategize

Now that you understand the reason to **recognize**, then to **initialize**, The next step is **Strategize to maximize.** To generate a high possibility of success, you must first establish a workable strategy. This phase is what I regard as the method's central tenet. If you don't have a strong, well-planned strategy, your chances of winning will probably be low.

How to Strategize to Achieve Your Goals?

> **It Starts with a Plan and Follows with More Plans**
> The concept of "Plan B" came into being from the idea that having more plans after the initial plan is necessary. A backup plan does not ensure you will always need one but certainly enhances the odds of your primary plan being

successful. Nevertheless, it is best to have a backup plan in case unforeseen obstacles arise. Instead of scrambling and giving up due to Plan A failing, having Plan B, C, or D will at least provide you with other alternatives that will keep you moving instead of stopping.

> **Focus and Discipline**
Concentration and self-control are two highly essential qualities required in any endeavor. Without these qualities, nothing, no matter how large or small the tasks, plans, or objectives may be, can ever be completed. Unfortunately, the environment is full of distractions, and these diversions come in a wide variety of types. Considering the advanced technological civilization that exists now, technology seems to be the source of the greatest number of diversions for most people of all ages. How many hours a day do you find yourself glued to your phone, monitoring social media and messaging on it? We are constantly barraged with information and various forms of entertainment, not only on the phone but other electronic devices that are merely a click away. Because of this, the bombardment is tough to avoid, unless one completely cuts away from these great innovations. Since it's almost impossible to avoid using technological advances, you may as well make the most of them by advancing your capabilities. Choose items to watch on YouTube™ that will inspire you in your subject rather than waste time viewing meaningless items. Find things that can help enhance your life and fuel your focus instead of reading about the lives of celebrities. Make use of apps to discipline yourself by setting a timer to remind you of tasks to do so that you don't get sidetracked. Be careful to identify what pulls you away from your target and what draws you closer to attaining achievement, regardless of whether the diversions you face are internal or external.

> **Break Goals into Small Chunks**
It takes time to reach your goal, and sometimes along the way, you might feel overwhelmed. Breaking your goals into chunks can help with inertia. Achieving one small goal along

the path to your destination allows you to create dopamine, a "feel-good" hormone. This sense of happiness allows you to keep momentum and look forward to achieving the next small goal. In addition to feeling good, having a goal divided into more manageable steps makes your focus much easier, which boosts confidence and motivation. Another benefit of breaking your goal into smaller chunks is that it allows you to evaluate your strengths and weaknesses so that you can change your strategies. When I authored my book, *Split Up by The Sea*, the goal was to publish it within the set time. However, several things I didn't consider were content editing, line editing, book cover design, formatting, beta readers' feedback, and finally publishing. I was consumed with getting the book done so I felt overwhelmed and slowed down my writing. That was when I decided to break these goals into chunks and give a deadline for each section. Once I acknowledged that I had to accomplish each one of these goals sequentially, I felt more at ease every time I started writing, and not long after, I was able to complete the biggest goal of my life, publishing my first memoir. When your mind is at peace and happy, nothing is impossible.

> **Create a Better Mood**
A positive frame of mind is essential to moving in the right direction. How often do you find yourself wanting to accomplish tasks but not being in the mood for them? It happens rather often, doesn't it? To attain a good mood, you need to have some upbeat emotions. What exactly do I mean by that?

Here is a list of four positive hormones as cited in Healthline.com/health/happy-hormone:

- o **Dopamine:** associated with pleasurable sensations, along with learning, memory, and more.

- o **Serotonin:** helps regulate your mood as well as your sleep, appetite, digestion, learning ability, and memory.

- o **Oxytocin:** promotes trust, empathy, and bonding in relationships.

- o **Endorphins:** a body's natural pain reliever in response to stress and discomfort.

Ways to produce these "happy hormones":

- o Engaging in outdoor activities is a must as sunlight increases serotonin. A moderate amount of physical activity, such as strolling around the neighborhood or trekking at a nearby lake a few times each week is sufficient. Also, breathing in the fresh air and taking in the sights outside is certain to lift your spirits. Remember to use sunscreen when going outside since exposure to UV rays may raise your chance of developing skin cancer.

- o Go to a gym or any available space for a workout. Exercising helps promote the increase of endorphins, dopamine, and serotonin.

- o Laughter is always the best medicine and it's free. Get together with friends and enjoy a friendly conversation. Laughter reduces anxiety and stress, thereby improving your mood by increasing dopamine and endorphin levels.

- o Cooking and eating in a family setting also helps with releasing dopamine and endorphins. In addition, spicy foods, foods high in tryptophan, or foods containing probiotics, can elevate happy hormones.

o

> **Avoid Procrastination**

Because it may act as a roadblock on the route to achievement, procrastination is likely one of the behaviors almost everyone wishes they could stop, but it's also one of the most difficult to break. When you allow yourself to be dominated by procrastination, a slow and steady death of goal accomplishment may result. If putting off tasks until they are close to a deadline or coming up with excuses to avoid them for as long as possible is something you do regularly, then now is the time to make a change. Furthermore, procrastination is a deeply entrenched pattern of behavior, meaning it is not simple to stop overnight. This makes it a challenge to overcome. One approach is to find someone as an accountability partner. Having someone remind you and enforce specific deadlines would make you feel guilty and influence you to finish your tasks.

> **Manage Your Time Effectively**

Have you ever heard of the condition known as "shiny squirrel syndrome?" It is an irrational response to what professionals refer to as "shiny objects." We all, without exception, have that natural inclination to investigate things that are novel and unfamiliar. On the other hand, curiosity about new things might influence you to follow different passions. My friend, Jackson, had an objective to launch a fitness center that specialized in providing only exercise machines. While he was waiting for renovations to be completed at his facility, he went to other gyms and became receptive to adding a boxing ring and a theater room with exercise cycles. Implementation of his first plan was slowed somewhat since he decided to include those new amenities in his workout space. As a direct consequence of this, not only was the opening date delayed, but he also spent more time and money than he originally anticipated.

> ➤ **Anticipate Obstacles and Failures**
> Failures and hurdles are not anyone's favorite things, but unfortunately, everyone has at least some experience with them. These failures are difficult to bear, and you most likely do not want to experience them again in your life. Regrettably, there is no assurance of that being the case. You may, however, train yourself to anticipate, which will decrease the impact of those unwelcome sensations. You will be prepared and know how to handle failures when they occur, so at least you won't go off course. You will be able to formulate a more robust plan and a more comprehensive approach if you accomplish this. You will be in a better position to adapt your strategy to account for new information. As you continue to strive towards your goal by anticipating obstacles and failures, you will be able to keep your spirit from diminishing.

13 Let's Energize

"The energy of the mind is the essence of life."

-ARISTOTLE

R.I.S.E. - Energize

The last part of this **R.I.S.E.** system is **Energize to capitalize**. When used in this sense, the word "energize" refers to the process of injecting a situation with energy or excitement. This is crucial because having a positive and proactive attitude may help you take advantage of opportunities and overcome problems. Having a positive and proactive attitude is vital. When you are energized, not only are you more likely to be focused and driven, but you also capitalize on the challenges you face.

On the other hand, if you are experiencing feelings of exhaustion, apathy, or discouragement, you may be less inclined to make the most of the possibilities when they present themselves. Additionally, there is a likelihood of being more prone to making errors or missing essential facts.

You will not be able to take action until you first find enthusiasm and energy in yourself. You are the driving force behind your existence. Your ability to retain energy for as long as you see fit is in your control. Think back to times when you were depressed, when all you wanted to do was be alone, or when you didn't have the energy to accomplish anything. How did you react? It was aggravating, wasn't it? You want to avoid being sidetracked from pursuing your goal at any cost. If you keep allowing low energy to normalize, you will almost certainly come to a full standstill. On the other end of the scale, try to remember a period in your life when you were full of vitality, excitement, and confidence to take on anything. You were shocked by all the things you were able to do. To be successful in achieving your goals, you need to have an optimistic, upbeat, and active mindset.

Have you ever seen the renowned motivational speakers Tony Robbins or Les Brown? Both speakers can be found on YouTube™. As they continue to converse, the inflections in their voices became much more pronounced. You could tell from their emotions that they were assessing the reactions of the audience while they were speaking. Even from where you were sitting, you could sense the thrill they were feeling. What is their secret to success? What type of power enables them to always have a positive attitude and be so full of life? The answer is energy, a lot of positive energy.

"Energy cannot be created or destroyed, it can only be changed from one form to another."

-ALBERT EINSTEIN

Ways to foster positive energy:

> **Keeping Your Body Healthy**
> To begin, it is necessary to maintain a healthy body. When the mind and the body are working in tandem, you will experience the greatest amount of vitality. This is another way high energy is created. Therefore, maintaining good states in both body and mind is equally crucial. It is a kind of collaboration, and one of the tenets of martial arts is that the mind and body must become one.

Ways to take care of the body:

- Your body needs rest, and to get that rest, sleeping is necessary. For your body to be able to fully recover throughout the day, experts recommend getting between seven and nine hours of sleep each night. However, since each person is unique, it is important to pay attention to your body. If you wake up after a long night and still feel tired, it may be a sign that your body requires more sleep or that there are underlying health concerns. For further information, discuss the matter with your physician. In addition, you could consider taking a nap as an alternative. I've found that having a quick nap of ten to fifteen minutes is helpful. Based on my experience, I don't think it's a good idea to snooze for more than thirty minutes at a time since it makes my body feel lethargic.

- The body gets many benefits from regular exercise. For five days a week, I work out with my students virtually, weightlifting for three days and karate on the other two days. You can strengthen your muscles to protect joints and ligaments by engaging in physical activity. In addition, feeling powerful and being strong will build up your self-esteem. However, be sure not to over-exercise the same muscles and allow time to recover. It is not suggested to work on the same muscle group daily as this could lead to injury since the muscle is being strained versus built-up.

- Stretching is another vital component. Although exercise is beneficial for building muscle, stretching is beneficial for maintaining mobility. Your ability to move freely will decrease as your muscles get tight and stiff. After that occurs, you won't have as much mobility, making it more challenging to carry out the tasks of daily living. Because you are slowly losing control over your body as you gradually age, this may also influence your emotions. Therefore, stretching for ten minutes every day might be beneficial.

- Consuming nutritious food will assist in maintaining the health of your body. Be sure to get the appropriate nutrients that are beneficial for your body and steer clear of foods that are high in saturated fat, sugar, and trans-fats. Instead, focus on eating foods that are low in these unhealthy components. Initially, consumption of these meals may provide you with a surge of energy; however, after a few hours, you may experience feelings of lethargy. Frequently select fruits, veggies, lean meats, and cereals that are whole grain. You will get the same surge from them, but without the withdrawal symptoms that arise later.

- Taking time off for oneself is yet another effective strategy for recharging one's batteries. There are going to be times when you feel exhausted or overwhelmed by events that are happening in your life or at work. Take a few minutes to relax and think about things on your own. Listening to music that you like might assist in putting your mind at ease. You could also find that writing in a notebook or meditating helps alleviate your stress.

> **Waking Up Early in the Morning**
I have always been enthused about why successful people tend to wake up early, and I wished that I had practiced this

routine when I was much younger. Studies have shown that your brain is most alert and active in the morning, which means you can accomplish more and work effectively in less time. When waking up early, you align your sleep cycle with the natural rhythm of the sun, which can regulate your mood. It is not a coincidence that successful people keep on moving up the ranks. They come in early to work and start their day with the least amount of distractions. They understand that most interruptions, such as phone calls, emails, or meetings, occur later in the day. Therefore, coming in early to work is a strategy to get things done and feel energized.

Years ago, when I lived in New York City, I noticed many elders practicing Tai Chi at 7 AM at various parks on the weekends. Out of curiosity, as I drove along the park, I approached a Tai Chi master and asked if I could participate. Joyfully, he welcomed me to the group and I followed along. It was amazing to see how Tai Chi was the total opposite of my karate training. Everything was slow and soft. My limbs were never tight and I had to consciously look at the motion of my arms and legs. After thirty minutes of practicing with the group, I found myself hooked on the art. Tai Chi is a martial art that teaches controlling the breath and movement of body. Essentially, the purpose of these movements was to control the energy throughout your entire body. Normally, Tai Chi is done in the early morning because it is believed the air is cleaner and it sets the tone for the day. This art became my early morning routine as it energized me and primed my mind with positivity for the entire day.

➢ **Surround Yourself with Fun People**
Surrounding yourself with fun people gives you energy because they make you laugh, smile, and enjoy life. Fun people are positive, optimistic, and adventurous. They inspire you to try new things, challenge yourself, and grow. They also support, encourage, and celebrate your achievements. When you are with fun people, you feel happier, more confident, and more motivated. They help you

recharge your batteries and cope with stress. Someone who is introverted may not like being in a large social gathering. However, introverts can have fun. If you are introverted, you can certainly be with one of your trusted friends who can make you laugh and allow you to share fun stories. When you feel energized with your friends, it extends to other areas of your life.

In 2010, fifteen of us recreational tennis players decided to form a team and play under the United States Tennis Association (USTA) organization. To start, we just wanted to have fun and be active. However, as we played, we earned an undefeated record and won the league that advanced us to the district level, then Sectional, which was one step away from National. It was never our intention to be that competitive. We just wanted to play and stay in shape. However, being surrounded by fun and inspiring people made us work harder during our practice sessions and we wanted to take our tennis to another level. Whenever we gathered to prepare for the Sectional tournament, we had fun motivating each other. On the day of the tournament, all of us played our hearts out. Unfortunately, we lost a close match but didn't feel disappointed at all. We gave our best effort and that was what counted. Most importantly, our group was filled with fun and inspiring people who helped bring out the best of us to compete at our highest level.

➢ **Learning to be Comfortable During Uncomfortable Situations**
The "comfort zone" is a place everyone strives to be in because they feel secure and confident. Is it the case, or is it another excuse to avoid confronting the issue? Being in a comfortable situation or doing comfortable activities for an extended period can eventually lead to boredom and unhappiness. As time passes, the fire that drives your needs will gradually die out, and you may question the purpose of your existence since you are unable to see the effects of your contribution. At this point, positive energy will be depleted. Therefore, to reignite that energy, you need to break out of

your comfort zone and try new experiences. You may be surprised to see an improved version of yourself by excelling in your personal development. Not only can expanding yourself provide delight, but it also has the potential to affirm the genuine worth that you possess. Now is the moment to put yourself in an "uncomfortable zone" and get used to being there. Instead of allowing the prospect of being awkward to get you down, redirect your attention to things you excel at doing. As soon as you alter how you view things, your energy will likewise shift. If you consider what advantages you can provide to others and what unique contributions you can make, you will be able to build up enough positive energy to overcome any obstacle.

➤ **Stop Wandering and Be in the Now**
You have the power to dream and fantasize about all the creative possibilities for your life. However, at some point, you will need to stop dreaming of the world of your imagination and start accepting the world of reality. Living in a universe in which everything unfolds in accordance with your wishes is always a pleasant experience, but it's all in your mind. Your mental health will suffer because of your inability to put a stop to this unrealistic world. In the end, you will suffer disappointment and dissatisfaction. The longer you remain in this condition, the less energy you will have to proceed. Keep your attention fixed on the here and now rather than allowing your thoughts to meander off to that fantastical place. Take pleasure in "being in the here and now" and be grateful for the things you possess. Therefore, you should refrain from worrying about matters over which you have no control. Focus your attention on things that you can do rather than ones that you are unable to perform. It is a waste of time and effort to continue trying to find a solution to an issue for which there is none. Spending time and effort on things that bring you down is a waste of both.

➤ **Fix Your Focus, Change Your Energy**
Fixing your focus on what can be done is a strategy that helps you overcome obstacles or stop dwelling on negative

thoughts. A Zen master once said to me, "Don't live your life in worry. If you can fix it, why worry? If you can't fix it, then what's the point of worrying?" I was at a loss for words, but he was right, and it gave me a distinct perspective on life. Why worry if there is a solution? And if there is no solution, worrying will not alleviate anything, but instead, rob you of happiness. Worrying is a waste of time which ends up bringing you no solution whatsoever. It makes you lose focus and leads to frustration and energy depletion.

A few years ago, I devised a three-day training program for independent inventors who wanted to know more about the patent filing and applying process. It took me at least six months to develop the training materials, including approval from upper management. I was excited about my finished product and couldn't wait to showcase it. Sadly, I was told that the program would not be merited if no more than twenty applicants applied for the program. I became anxious and constantly checked to see how many applicants registered. Then I remembered what the Zen master said to me. Why worry about things I have no control over? Instead of wasting time worrying, I should be more proactive in marketing. I fixed my focus. I modified my marketing materials, sent out more information about the program, and hoped to pique more interest. While changing the marketing strategy, my energy level also changed. In each meeting that I had with my team, I constantly reminded them, "We can do this!" They felt the excitement that I exuded and knew how important this program meant to me. What made this process more profound was that my focus was solely on doing the best that I could versus being stressed out if the outcome did not go in my favor. After a month, I was overjoyed with the number of participants who registered. It was triple the enrollment requirement!

14 R.I.S.E. to Reap

"An idea not coupled with action will never get any bigger than the brain cell it occupied."

-ARNOLD H. GLASOW

Putting Into Action

YOu've been introduced to the **R.I.S.E.** (**Recognize. Initialize. Strategize. Energize**) system. It's time to put things into action and reap the benefits. Remember, nothing comes to fruition unless you start moving. So, let's RISE.

The gist of this book is to break the bricks, face the obstacles ahead of you, and prepare to knock them down. Often, people wish to go back in time with the knowledge they have now to execute a plan that they had. Worst yet, they think, "It's too late for me to do something now," which I often hear. Well, don't let this be you!

Let's face reality and start putting the **R.I.S.E.** system to work. Certainly, there will be no magic wand to send you back and change anything. Most importantly, you should never allow yourself to contemplate that it is too late to start something new. It is only late when you choose to stay still and complain. It's time to move if you have that burning desire to do the things you love. Opportunities come and go as we progress in life. I am a believer that once you manifest your thoughts and send them to the universe, good fortune will return to you. The question here is, will you be prepared to accept and face the challenge to reap the benefit? The universe is fair, it doesn't hand you the result but only provides the path and opportunity. You are the one to create the result by putting in your best effort.

The road to success can be bumpy. Nevertheless, face it head-on and find ways to move forward despite what is in front of you. If you are willing to accept challenges, your willingness will bring you one step closer to realizing your ambitions. Train yourself not to be intimidated by obstacles by having a positive attitude that everything will be alright. When you envision that the sky is the limit, you will try every means to get there. You have more strength of determination than you give yourself credit for. The more you learn to control it, the greater the number of miracles you will be able to achieve.

I am a firm believer in the adage "Where there's a will, there's a way." This is how I persisted in my efforts and accomplished what I desired throughout my life. When you have a strong will, it appears as if the world works in your favor, opening all doors and providing you with more opportunities to achieve your goals.

I believe that there are two types of people, complacent and doer. I predict you are a doer, otherwise, this book wouldn't reach your hands and be read through to the last chapter. For a doer, there is only one choice when obstacles are present, and that is having a mindset that difficulties are there to instruct you, not to obstruct you. In any case, you want to be proud and say, "At least I tried it," instead of regretting never having tried.

I hope that the life lessons and struggles I have learned and encountered have inspired you. Along with the **R.I.S.E.** (**Recognize. Initialize. Strategize. Energize.**) system you will be motivated to break your own bricks (obstacles) and discover your full potential. Remember, rise to the opportunity and take chances! The last thing you want is to regret not capitalizing on the opportunity. You need to adopt a different mentality and see barriers as growth. Each difficulty that you conquer brings you one step closer to achieving your goals.

As you implement the **R.I.S.E.** system into your success, it is vital to believe in yourself. Indeed, your loved ones will always love you, but they will not believe in you unless you believe in yourself. When you agree to start something, you also need to hold yourself accountable by sticking to the plan throughout the entire journey. Of course, during your journey, there will be those who say things to hurt and hinder you from progressing, but it is up to you to choose whether to listen to them or not. You cannot control what people say, but you can control what you want to hear. Surely, the path to success is not easy, but it doesn't mean you cannot get there. I have shown and taught the **R.I.S.E.** system to many students, clients, and employees, and the results have been astounding. I have seen many individuals transform their lives and find happiness because they finally realized their true potential after breaking through that invisible wall.

I wish you all success in achieving your next dream. Apply all that willpower that resides in you to make your dreams and goals come true. Lastly, go back to this book whenever you find yourself in a rut. Your true power is on the other side of the bricks. Go ahead and Break the Bricks!!!

Afterword on Fear and Breaking Obstacles

As humans, we all go through life meeting challenges, some of which are more significant than others. You often find yourself living in fear, terrified to take the first step toward conquering these obstacles because you are fearful of what could happen if you do. The real fear, though, comes from seeing other people achieve success in ways that you, too, might have conducted if you had taken the necessary steps. ***You succumb to fear because your plan is not clear!***

Living a life filled with regret is a difficult weight to carry. You do not want to spend the rest of your life wondering what could have been and how much your life may have been altered had you tried to make anything happen. However, the fear of failing or of the unknown may be paralyzing, making it difficult to take that first step toward your goals.

In this book, I presented you with ideas that will aid you in overcoming your fear and engaging in activities that are needed to move forward. I am optimistic that you will be able to use the tools I have provided to effectively use in your own life and that they will make it much easier for you to implement choices to move ahead.

Keep in mind that worrying is often a consequence of not having a clear strategy. When you are unsure of what you want or how to get there, you tend to feel cautious and fearful of taking action. You will be able to go ahead with assurance and knowledge that you are on the right path if you first make an effort to define your goals and formulate a strategy.

I hope you found this book illuminating as an instructive companion on your path toward conquering challenges and realizing your ambitions. Keep in mind that the only thing preventing you from achieving success is fear, and if you have the correct mentality and proper tools, you can conquer it.

ABOUT THE AUTHOR

I hope you enjoyed this book. Please consider writing a review to help other readers enjoy **Break the Bricks**. Thank you!

Want to know more about Len Tran's next project?
Follow the author on social media!

https://www.facebook.com/len.tran.7106
https://www.linkedin.com/in/len-tran
https://www.LenVTran.com

Len Tran was born in Hue, in the region of Central Vietnam, and immigrated to the United States in 1982. After receiving a Chemical Engineering degree from City College of New York in 1998, he worked for the Department of Environmental Protection in New York City and then later moved to Virginia to establish his career at the United States Patent and Trademark Office. Len is a speaker, trainer, and a life coach at Kinetic Mind, LLC. His goal is to inspire and engage his audience with techniques that will make them **R.I.S.E.** from their seats.